TILL
BETRAYAL
Do Us
PART

A Memoir of Surviving Narcissistic Abuse

Study Guide

CHERYL DYSON-BENNETT

Designed for Greatness Publishing
Atlanta, Georgia
https://greatnesscoachingandconsulting.com/en-us/
Elevate Your Leadership Journey

CONTENTS

INTRODUCTION
TILL BETRAYAL DO US PART: AN INVITATION TO UNDERSTAND AND HEAL

Welcome to Till Betrayal Do Us Part: A Memoir of Surviving Narcissistic Abuse Study Guide. This guide is designed to accompany your exploration of the powerful and poignant memoir that sheds light on the often-hidden struggles of navigating life with a narcissistic partner. Whether you are a survivor, a supporter, or simply someone seeking understanding, this study book offers a path to deeper comprehension and healing through collective reflection and discussion.

THE POWER OF SHARED EXPERIENCES

Narcissistic abuse is a profoundly isolating experience, one that can leave emotional scars and create a sense of disconnection from one's own sense of self. This memoir, however, is more than just a personal story; it is a testament to resilience, recovery, and the power of community. By coming together to study and discuss this memoir, we create a space where voices can be heard, experiences can be validated, and healing can begin.

WHAT THIS STUDY GUIDE OFFERS

In the chapters that follow, you will find a series of thoughtfully crafted discussion questions and reflective exercises designed to enhance your understanding of the memoir and its themes. This study guide aims to:

Deepen Your Understanding: Each question is intended to prompt a thorough examination of the memoir's key themes, such as the dynamics of narcissistic abuse, the journey to self-recovery, and the importance of setting boundaries. By engaging with these questions, you will gain a richer understanding of the memoir's content and its broader implications.

Facilitate Meaningful Discussions: The discussion questions are designed to provoke thoughtful dialogue, whether in a group setting or through individual reflection. They encourage participants to share their personal insights, explore different perspectives, and connect the memoir's themes to their own experiences.

Promote Emotional Healing: Navigating the terrain of narcissistic abuse can be challenging and emotional. This guide provides a structured approach to process your feelings, find support, and take steps toward healing. Through reflective questions and group discussions, you will have the opportunity to confront your own experiences and work towards emotional resolution.

HOW TO USE THIS GUIDE

To make the most of this study book, consider the following approach:

1. **Familiarize Yourself with the Memoir**: Before diving into the discussion questions, read the memoir thoroughly to grasp its narrative, themes, and emotional depth. Familiarity with the content will enhance your engagement with the study questions.

2. **Engage with the Questions**: Approach each discussion question with an open mind. Take time to reflect on your responses and consider how they connect with the memoir's themes. If you are in a group setting, listen to others' perspectives and share your own insights openly.

3. **Document Your Journey**: Keep a personal journal or notes on your reflections and the discussions you participate in. This will help you track your progress, uncover new insights, and remember key takeaways from each session.

4. **Apply Your Learnings**: Use the insights gained from this study to inform your personal growth and healing journey. Reflect on how the memoir and discussions resonate with your own experiences and explore practical steps to foster your recovery.

EMBARKING ON A JOURNEY OF UNDERSTANDING

This study guide is more than a collection of questions—it is an invitation to embark on a journey of understanding and healing. By engaging with the memoir and participating in the discussions, you are taking a significant step toward reclaiming your sense of self and finding solace in shared experiences.

We hope this guide serves as a valuable companion in your exploration of *Till Betrayal Do Us Part*, and that it supports you in navigating the complexities of narcissistic abuse with empathy, strength, and resilience.

Thank you for joining us on this journey. May your exploration be enlightening, your discussions enriching, and your path to healing profound.

JOURNEY THROUGH TURMOIL: THE SHATTERED FAÇADE OF LOVE

This chapter sets the foundation for understanding the protagonist's tumultuous journey through narcissistic abuse, focusing on two distinct but interrelated aspects of the relationship.

SECTION 1: INITIAL REALIZATION AND RECOGNITION OF NARCISSISTIC ABUSE

In this section, the narrative introduces readers to the early stages of recognizing narcissistic abuse. The protagonist begins to identify the manipulative and emotionally damaging behaviors exhibited by their partner. Key elements include:

1. **Initial Awareness**: The protagonist starts to notice the telltale signs of narcissistic abuse, including emotional manipulation and a pattern of self-serving behavior from their partner.

2. **Emotional Impact**: There is a growing awareness of how these abusive behaviors are affecting the protagonist's self-esteem, mental health, and overall well-being, leading to a profound emotional impact.

3. **Denial and Confusion**: The protagonist grapples with the complexity of their emotions, including denial and confusion, as they struggle to accept the reality of the abuse and its implications for their relationship.

4. **Personal Reflection**: Reflection on past experiences within the relationship provides deeper insights into the dynamics of the abuse, setting the stage for understanding the full scope of the partner's narcissistic behavior.

SECTION 2: ESCALATING DISSONANCE AND BETRAYAL

This section delves into the increasing dissonance and betrayal within the relationship, marked by the husband's erratic and deceptive behavior. The key themes include:

1. **Behavioral Inconsistency**: The husband's sudden change in behavior—such as performing household chores—creates confusion, contrasting sharply with his usual neglect and detachment.

2. **Emotional Distance**: Despite these outward actions, the husband remains emotionally aloof and gives the protagonist the silent treatment, exacerbating feelings of isolation and rejection.

3. **Secrecy and Deception:** The husband's growing secrecy, particularly regarding his phone and whereabouts, fuels the protagonist's anxiety and suspicion, indicating deeper issues within the marriage.

4. **Failure to Connect:** Efforts to reconnect through physical affection or meaningful conversations are met with rejection, highlighting the widening emotional gap between them.

5. **Unfulfilled Promises and Values:** The protagonist reflects on the erosion of shared values and promises, contrasting the husband's actions with the integrity and commitment they once valued.

6. **Impact of Betrayal:** The revelation of the husband's infidelity represents a profound breach of trust, shattering the protagonist's perception of their marriage and intensifying the emotional fallout.

Overall, Chapter 1 provides a compelling introduction to the memoir, illustrating the protagonist's initial realization of narcissistic abuse and the subsequent betrayal experienced in their relationship. It sets the stage for a deeper exploration of survival and resilience amidst the challenges of dealing with a narcissistic partner.

DISCUSSION QUESTIONS

1. Personal Impact of Unexpected Events:

– How did the unexpected request from the author's husband impact her emotional state on a day that was supposed to be focused on her book promotion?

– Can you recall a time when an unexpected personal or family issue disrupted an important event or goal in your own life? How did you handle it?

2. Communication in Relationships:

– What do you think might have led to the husband's request for a separation list? How does this reflect on their communication dynamics?

– How important is open and honest communication in relationships, especially during times of crisis? What strategies can be used to improve communication in a strained relationship?

3. Support and Blame:

– How did the author react to her husband's misplaced blame for his job loss and subsequent challenges? What are the potential effects of such blame on both individuals involved?

– In times of stress and difficulty, how can partners support each other without falling into patterns of blame or resentment?

4. Financial Strain and Marriage:

– Discuss the impact of financial strain on the author's marriage. How can financial stress affect relationships, and what can couples do to manage this stress together?

— What are some effective ways to address and alleviate financial concerns in a family setting?

5. Personal Growth and Resilience:

— How did the author's decision to support her husband in starting his own business reflect her values of selflessness and resilience?

— Can you share a personal experience where you had to demonstrate resilience and support for someone close to you? How did this experience contribute to your personal growth?

6. Dealing with Substance Abuse:

— The narrative mentions increasing use of alcohol and drugs by the author's husband. What are the potential signs of substance abuse, and how should one approach this sensitive issue?

— What resources or strategies can be utilized to support someone struggling with substance abuse, while also taking care of one's own well-being?

7. Coping with Emotional Distress:

— How did the author cope with her husband's emotional and behavioral changes, and what might have been the psychological toll on her?

— What are some healthy coping mechanisms for dealing with emotional distress in a family setting?

8. Trust and Transparency in Relationships:

- How did the husband's lack of transparency and sudden trips impact the author's trust in him? What are the potential effects of secrecy on a relationship?

- Can you share an experience where transparency (or the lack thereof) played a crucial role in your relationship dynamics? How was the situation resolved?

9. Handling Financial Strain

- How did the financial strain of the family influence the author's feelings about her husband's decisions? What are some strategies for managing financial stress within a relationship?

- Have you ever faced financial challenges in your relationships? How did you and your partner navigate these challenges?

10. Communication and Emotional Distance:

- How did the husband's behavior, such as his aloofness and refusal to engage emotionally, affect the author's sense of connection and intimacy? What are the signs of emotional distancing in a relationship?

- Discuss ways to address and improve communication when one partner is emotionally distant. What approaches have worked for you or others you know?

11. Dealing with Suspicion and Intuition:

- The author's intuition about her husband's behavior led her to question his actions and motives. How should one balance intuition and evidence when dealing with suspicions in a relationship?

– Have you ever had to confront someone based on your intuition or suspicions? How did you approach the situation, and what was the outcome?

12. Changes in Behavior and Relationship Dynamics:

– The husband's sudden willingness to help around the house and his changing behavior seemed suspicious to the author. How do sudden or unexplained changes in behavior affect your perception of someone's intentions?

– Can you think of a time when a significant change in someone's behavior led to a deeper understanding or revelation? How did it impact your relationship?

13. Privacy and Boundaries:

– How did the husband's increased secrecy around his phone affect the author's sense of security in the relationship? What are healthy boundaries when it comes to privacy and personal devices in a partnership?

– Discuss the importance of balancing privacy and transparency in a relationship. What boundaries should be set to ensure both partners feel secure and respected?

14. Emotional and Psychological Impact:

– The author mentioned feeling isolated and desolate despite her efforts to maintain the relationship. How can prolonged emotional neglect or distance affect one's mental health and well-being?

– What self-care practices or support systems can help individuals cope with emotional and psychological strain in their relationships?

15. Reflecting on Relationship Patterns:

– The author reflects on how the relationship had become more functional than passionate. How can couples recognize and address shifts in their relationship dynamics before they become detrimental?

– What are some signs that a relationship is shifting from a passionate connection to a more functional partnership, and how can these signs be addressed?

These questions are designed to explore the complexities of relationship dynamics, trust, communication, and personal boundaries as depicted in the narrative. They provide a framework for discussing similar experiences and strategies for managing relationship challenges.

16. Seeking Divine Intervention:

– The author prayed intensely for her marriage and felt that God wasn't listening. How do you cope with feelings of spiritual abandonment during personal crises? How can faith and prayer play a role in managing such feelings?

– Have you ever faced a situation where you felt your prayers or spiritual efforts were not answered as you hoped? How did you navigate that period?

17. Mismatch Between Words and Actions:

– The author struggled with her husband's actions not matching his words. How do you handle situations where someone's words do not align with their actions? What strategies can help bridge the gap between promises and behavior in relationships?

– Can you share an experience where someone's actions contradicted their words? How did it impact your relationship with them?

18. Feeling Out of Place:

– The author felt out of place during social gatherings with her husband's friends. How can individuals maintain their sense of self when feeling disconnected from the social circles of their partners?

– Discuss a time when you felt out of place or unsupported in a social setting related to your partner. How did you address these feelings?

19. Respect and Infatuation:

– The author observed her husband's inappropriate behavior towards another woman. How should one address and confront issues of disrespect and infidelity in a relationship?

– What are some effective ways to communicate feelings of hurt or betrayal when you observe inappropriate behavior from a partner?

20. Behavior Changes and Isolation:

– The author noted significant changes in her husband's behavior, including increased isolation and secrecy. How can couples identify and address sudden or concerning changes in behavior?

– Share an instance where you or someone you know experienced a sudden change in behavior. How was it addressed, and what was the outcome?

21. The Impact of Public Perception:

- The author's husband reacted negatively to the book's portrayal of their relationship, impacting his pride and public perception. How can couples navigate differences in how they want their relationship to be perceived publicly versus privately?

- Have you encountered a situation where public perception of your personal life affected your relationship? How did you handle it?

22. Dealing with Infidelity

- The author discovered her husband's infidelity and struggled with feelings of betrayal and trust. What are some steps to take when faced with infidelity in a relationship? How can one rebuild trust after such a breach?

- Discuss a time when trust was broken in a relationship you are familiar with. How was the situation managed, and what was the impact on the relationship?

23. Personal Growth Through Adversity:

- Despite the challenges in her marriage, the author found purpose in writing her book. How can personal adversity lead to personal growth and new opportunities?

- Can you share an experience where a personal challenge led to unexpected growth or a new path in your life?

24. Balancing Emotional Responses:

- The author's emotional response to her husband's betrayal was intense, ranging from anger to profound sadness. How can one balance emotional responses with practical steps in dealing with betrayal or personal crisis?

– How do you manage your emotions when faced with overwhelming or painful situations? What strategies have helped you maintain a sense of balance?

25. Revisiting Core Values:

– The author reflects on her values and how they contrasted with her husband's actions. How can couples ensure they remain aligned with their core values, especially during challenging times?

– Discuss a time when you or someone you know had to reassess or realign with core values in a relationship. What was the process, and how did it affect the relationship?

These questions are intended to facilitate a deep and meaningful discussion about the themes of faith, trust, communication, and personal growth reflected in your narrative.

REFLECTIVE EXERCISE:
RECOGNIZING PATTERNS AND EMOTIONS

PURPOSE:

To encourage readers to explore their own experiences with relationships, identify patterns similar to those described in the memoir, and reflect on their emotional responses.

INSTRUCTIONS:

1. Journaling Prompt:

– Reflect on a time when you felt confusion or denial in a relationship. Write about the specific behaviors or events that led you to feel this way. Consider the following questions:

– What were the signs you noticed that made you question the health of the relationship?

– How did you justify or rationalize these behaviors at the time?

– Did you experience any emotional shifts similar to those described in the chapter (e.g., changes in self-esteem, feelings of isolation)?

2. Identifying Patterns:

– Create a list of behaviors in past relationships that now feel familiar. Write down instances of emotional manipulation, inconsistency, or betrayal you experienced or observed. Reflect on:

– How did these patterns affect your emotional well-being?

— Were there moments when you felt compelled to overlook or minimize these behaviors? What influenced that decision?

3. Emotional Mapping:

— Draw a simple emotional map. Start by writing "My Relationship Experience" in the center. Branch out with different emotions you felt during your most challenging relationship experiences (e.g., confusion, sadness, anger, hope).

— For each emotion, write a few sentences describing a specific memory or moment that triggered it.

4. Setting Intentions:

— After reflecting on these experiences, write a short paragraph about what you hope to understand or achieve through this study guide. Consider:

— How can recognizing these patterns and feelings contribute to your healing journey?

— What boundaries or changes would you like to implement in your future relationships?

5. Discussion Sharing (Optional):

— If in a group setting, consider sharing one insight from your reflections that resonated with you. This could be a behavior pattern you identified or a specific emotion you wish to explore further.

CLOSING:

As you complete this reflective exercise, remember that understanding and healing is often a journey filled with ups and downs. Revisiting your reflections periodically can help you deepen your insights and foster personal growth. Recognizing these patterns is a vital step in reclaiming your sense of self and cultivating healthier relationships moving forward. Be gentle with yourself as you navigate this process, and know that every step you take brings you closer to healing and empowerment.

NOTES

_____

_____

_____

_____

_____

_____

_____

_____

_____

_____

_____

_____

_____

NOTES

NOTES

NOTES

NOTES

_____

_____

_____

_____

_____

_____

_____

_____

_____

_____

_____

_____

_____

2

EMBRACING SACRIFICIAL LOVE: TRIALS, LESSONS, AND A QUEST FOR FREEDOM

This chapter focuses on the theme of sacrificial love and the personal trials and lessons associated with it. The chapter reflects the protagonist's journey through embracing a deep, selfless love while navigating the complexities of a troubled marriage.

CENTRAL THEME: SACRIFICIAL LOVE AND PERSONAL REFLECTION

1. **Sacrificial Love**: The chapter opens with the protagonist preparing to speak at an event, drawing from a profound sense of sacrificial love inspired by their faith. This type of love involves prioritizing the needs and emotions of others, mirroring the unconditional love exemplified by

Jesus Christ. The protagonist reflects on biblical teachings about love and self-sacrifice, emphasizing that true love is demonstrated through actions and empathy, not just words.

2. Challenges in Marriage: Despite the protagonist's commitment to sacrificial love, they face significant challenges in their marriage. The chapter discusses their efforts to embody this love through forgiveness and prayer, despite feeling that their pleas for a better relationship seem unanswered. The protagonist's fervent prayers for their husband and the marriage are contrasted with the ongoing struggles and perceived lack of divine intervention.

3. Personal Struggle and Growth: The protagonist grapples with feelings of failure and disappointment in their marriage. They reflect on their personal growth and the bittersweet realization of their efforts not leading to the desired outcome. This reflection is intertwined with their faith journey, as they question whether their marriage is serving God's purpose or if it is time for change.

4. Biblical Parallels and Reflection: The chapter draws parallels between the protagonist's situation and the biblical story of the Israelites' escape from slavery under Pharaoh. The protagonist compares their struggles to the Israelites' quest for freedom, pondering whether their marital difficulties are symbolic of a larger barrier to spiritual and personal freedom.

5. Pruning and Renewal: The chapter concludes with the idea of divine pruning, where God removes parts of our lives that no longer bear fruit to allow for growth and renewal. The protagonist reflects on the possibility that their marriage, as it stands, may not be fulfilling its intended purpose and may need to be let go for new growth to occur.

Overall, Chapter 2 explores the complexities of practicing sacrificial love within a troubled marriage, the emotional and spiritual trials involved, and the quest for personal and relational freedom. It blends personal reflection with biblical teachings, emphasizing the tension between enduring love and the need for transformative change.

DISCUSSION QUESTIONS

1. Understanding Sacrificial Love:

– The chapter discusses sacrificial love as a form of love that goes beyond mere words and actions. How do you understand the concept of sacrificial love in the context of your relationships? Can you share an example from your life where sacrificial love was demonstrated?

– How can sacrificial love be practiced in daily life, especially when dealing with challenging situations or conflicts?

2. Living Out Biblical Love:

– 1 Corinthians 13:4-7 describes the attributes of love. Which of these attributes do you find most challenging to embody, and why? How can you work on integrating these attributes into your relationships?

– Reflect on the verse from Mark 12:30-31 about loving God and loving your neighbor. How can prioritizing these commandments impact your approach to loving others sacrificially?

3. The Role of Prayer in Relationships:

– The author mentioned the importance of prayer in seeking change and guidance in her marriage. How do you incorporate prayer into your own relationships or personal struggles? What role has prayer played in your life during difficult times?

– Have you experienced a situation where prayer significantly impacted the outcome of a relationship or personal challenge? How did it help?

4. Forgiveness and Its Challenges:

— Forgiving someone who has wronged you can be incredibly difficult. What are some practical steps you can take to forgive others, even when it feels hard or unjust?

— How does the principle of forgiveness, as mentioned in Matthew 6:14-15, influence your interactions with others? Can you share a time when forgiveness was a key factor in resolving a conflict?

5. Facing Personal Trials and Growth:

— The author likened her struggles to the Israelites' journey and the concept of divine pruning. How do you perceive personal trials as opportunities for growth? What are some ways you've seen personal challenges lead to positive change in your life?

— Reflect on John 15:1-2 about pruning. What "dead weight" might you need to let go of in your life to grow spiritually or personally?

6. The Quest for Freedom:

— The chapter discusses feeling trapped and seeking freedom from oppressive situations. How do you identify when you are feeling trapped in a situation, and what steps can you take to seek freedom or change?

— Can you relate to the idea of "Pharaoh" as an obstacle in your life? How do you confront and overcome such obstacles to find liberation or a sense of purpose?

7. Balancing Personal Goals and Relationship Needs:

- The author struggled with balancing her personal goals and the needs of her marriage. How do you balance pursuing personal goals while also nurturing and supporting your relationships?

- Discuss a time when you had to make a choice between personal aspirations and relationship needs. How did you navigate that decision?

8. Empathy and Compassion:

- The chapter emphasizes the importance of empathy and compassion in sacrificial love. How can you cultivate greater empathy and compassion in your interactions with others?

- Share an experience where empathy or compassion made a significant difference in a relationship or situation you were involved in.

9. Responding to Divine Guidance:

- The author sought divine guidance and struggled with feelings of unanswered prayers. How do you discern and respond to what you believe is divine guidance in your life?

- How do you stay encouraged and faithful when you feel that your prayers or desires are not being answered in the way you hoped?

10. Reflection on Personal Growth:

– The chapter reflects on personal growth and the bittersweet realization of progress amid ongoing struggles. How do you celebrate personal growth while acknowledging the areas that still need work?

– Discuss a moment of personal growth that was accompanied by a challenge or struggle. How did you reconcile the progress with the ongoing difficulties?

These questions aim to facilitate meaningful discussions about love, prayer, forgiveness, personal growth, and overcoming obstacles as reflected in the chapter.

REFLECTIVE EXERCISE:
EXPLORING SACRIFICIAL LOVE AND PERSONAL GROWTH

PURPOSE:

To encourage readers to reflect on their own experiences of love and sacrifice, identify personal struggles, and consider paths toward growth and renewal.

INSTRUCTIONS:

1. Journaling Prompt:

- Reflect on your own understanding of sacrificial love. Write about a time when you prioritized someone else's needs over your own. Consider the following questions:

- What motivated you to act selflessly in that situation?

- How did this experience impact your emotional well-being?

- Were there any feelings of resentment or disappointment afterward? Why or why not?

2. Assessing Challenges:

- Identify a current or past relationship where you felt your efforts at love and support were not reciprocated. Write about:

- The specific challenges you faced in that relationship.

- How your attempts at forgiveness and understanding were received.

- Any moments of realization or growth that emerged from those challenges.

3. Faith and Reflection:

– Reflect on your own faith or belief system and how it shapes your understanding of love and sacrifice. Write about:

– A teaching or principle that has influenced your approach to relationships.

– How this teaching has helped or hindered your personal growth in difficult situations.

4. Freedom and Letting Go:

– Consider the concept of "divine pruning" in your life. Reflect on areas where you feel stuck or unfulfilled. Write about:

– What aspects of your life or relationships may need to change or be let go to allow for new growth.

– How does the idea of letting go make you feel? What fears or hopes arise when you think about this process?

5. Setting Intentions for Growth:

– Write a short paragraph outlining one actionable step you can take toward your personal growth or relational freedom. Consider:

– What boundaries might you need to establish?

– How can you practice self-care while continuing to support others?

– What new opportunities for connection or healing can you explore?

6. Discussion Sharing (Optional):

— In a group setting, share one insight from your reflections that resonates with you. This could be a personal realization about sacrificial love, a lesson learned from past struggles, or an intention for future growth.

CLOSING:

As you wrap up this exercise, take a moment to appreciate the complexities of sacrificial love and how they shape your journey. Acknowledge that personal growth often emerges from challenges and deep reflection. By identifying areas for change and setting clear intentions, you empower yourself to pursue freedom and renewal in your life and relationships. Be gentle with yourself as you navigate this path and remember that growth is a gradual process. Each step you take brings you closer to understanding and fulfillment.

NOTES

NOTES

_____

_____

_____

_____

_____

_____

_____

_____

_____

_____

_____

_____

_____

NOTES

NOTES

NOTES

NOTES

LEARNING TO PRAY, TRUST & OBEY

This chapter delves into the theme of learning to pray, trust, and obey amid a turbulent marital situation. This chapter emphasizes the protagonist's deepening relationship with God as they navigate the challenges of their marriage and seek divine guidance.

CENTRAL THEME: THE POWER OF PRAYER, TRUST IN DIVINE GUIDANCE, AND THE CALL TO OBEDIENCE

1. **Seeking Solace in Prayer:** The chapter begins with the protagonist's struggle to find comfort and clarity through journaling and prayer. They turn to God as a confidant and source of strength, expressing their deepest frustrations and concerns about their marriage.

This personal dialogue with God becomes a crucial part of their journey, reflecting a growing dependence on divine guidance and support.

2. Heartfelt Pleas and Struggles: The protagonist shares their earnest and heartfelt prayers, revealing their emotional exhaustion and sense of betrayal. They grapple with feelings of unfulfilled expectations and a longing for a more meaningful and fulfilling relationship. These prayers express their desire for divine intervention and answers to their questions about their husband's behavior and their own role in the relationship.

3. Trusting in God's Plan: Despite their frustration and weariness, the protagonist expresses a deep trust in God's plan and timing. They recognize the need to rely on divine wisdom and seek reassurance from God, believing that their prayers will eventually lead to clarity and resolution. This trust is central to their ability to endure and continue their journey.

4. Obedience and Acceptance: The chapter highlights the protagonist's struggle with the concept of obedience—both to God and within their marriage. They contemplate whether their marital challenges are part of a larger divine plan and whether obedience might involve letting go of their current situation to embrace a new path. This reflection underscores the complexity of balancing personal desires with spiritual obedience.

5. Desire for Change and Fulfillment: The protagonist's prayers reflect a deep desire for change, both in their marriage and in their personal life. They express a longing for a relationship characterized by mutual respect, love, and shared values. The chapter closes with a poignant acknowledgment of the need to possibly let go of their husband for the sake of their own happiness and well-being.

In summary, Chapter 3 of Till Betrayal Do Us Part explores the transformative power of prayer, the importance of trusting in God's guidance, and the challenge of obedience in the face of personal struggles. It captures the protagonist's emotional journey as they seek divine clarity and support, ultimately wrestling with the difficult decision of whether to continue in their current relationship or embrace a new path.

DISCUSSION QUESTIONS

1. The Role of Prayer in Personal Struggles:

– The chapter highlights the author's reliance on prayer during times of distress. How do you personally approach prayer when facing significant challenges? What are some specific prayers or strategies that have been effective for you?

– How do you discern when you are hearing God's voice in your prayers? Share an experience where you felt your prayers were answered or guided you in a particular way.

2. Trusting God Amidst Uncertainty:

– The author expressed deep frustration and questions about her husband's behavior and the state of her marriage. How do you maintain trust in God when you are struggling with unanswered prayers or difficult circumstances?

– Reflect on a time when trusting God was particularly challenging. What steps did you take to continue trusting Him, and how did it impact your situation?

3. Obeying God's Will:

– The chapter discusses the struggle between personal desires and obedience to God's will. How do you determine whether you are acting in accordance with God's will in your life?

– Can you share an instance where you had to make a decision that required obedience to God's guidance, even though it was difficult or went against your initial desires?

4. Emotional Expression and Spiritual Growth:

– The author's journal entries express a range of emotions and frustrations. How can openly expressing our emotions, even in prayer, contribute to spiritual growth and understanding?

– Discuss the balance between expressing our frustrations and maintaining faith in God's plan. How can you ensure that your emotional expressions lead to constructive outcomes rather than despair?

5. Finding Solace in Journaling:

– Journaling was a significant part of the author's process. How does journaling or another form of reflective practice help you in your spiritual journey? What benefits have you experienced from this practice?

– What other methods do you use to process your emotions and seek guidance from God? How do these methods compare to the author's experience with journaling?

6. Handling Frustrations in Relationships:

– The chapter describes intense frustrations related to the author's marriage. How do you handle frustrations in your own relationships while trying to maintain a loving and constructive approach?

– What are some effective ways to address relationship issues with empathy and understanding, while also seeking resolution or improvement?

7. Desire for Change and Seeking Guidance:

– The author prayed for significant changes in her life and marriage. How do you approach seeking guidance for major life changes? What role does prayer play in making such decisions?

– Discuss a time when you felt a strong desire for change in your life. How did you seek guidance, and what were the outcomes of your efforts?

8. Balancing Self-Worth and Sacrificial Love:

– The chapter reflects on feelings of self-worth and the desire for a fulfilling life. How can you balance understanding your own value with the call to sacrificial love in relationships?

– How do you ensure that your desire for a fulfilling life and self-respect aligns with the biblical principles of love and service?

9. Understanding and Accepting God's Timing:

– The author grappled with the timing of God's response to her prayers. How do you reconcile with God's timing when it does not align with your expectations?

– Share an experience where waiting for God's timing taught you something important. How did you cope with the delay or uncertainty?

10. Encouragement and Support from Others:

– The chapter ends with a plea for encouragement. How can you offer support and encouragement to others who are struggling with similar issues?

— Discuss the importance of community and support in navigating personal and spiritual challenges. How can you build or contribute to a supportive network in your life?

These questions aim to foster deep reflection and discussion on themes of prayer, trust, obedience, and personal growth as highlighted in Chapter 3.

REFLECTIVE EXERCISE: EXPLORING PRAYER, TRUST, AND OBEDIENCE

PURPOSE:

To encourage readers to deepen their understanding of prayer, reflect on their relationship with faith, and consider how trust and obedience manifest in their lives.

INSTRUCTIONS:

1. Journaling Prompt:

— Reflect on your own experiences with prayer. Write about a time when you turned to prayer during a difficult situation. Consider the following questions:

— What prompted you to seek solace through prayer?

— How did you express your thoughts and feelings to God during that time?

— What answers or insights, if any, did you receive through this practice?

2. Identifying Struggles:

— Think about a challenge you currently face or have faced in the past where you felt a disconnect between your desires and your spiritual path. Write about:

— The specific feelings of frustration, disappointment, or confusion you experienced.

— How these feelings affected your trust in God or your willingness to obey His guidance.

3. Trusting the Process:

— Reflect on a time when you had to trust in a plan that felt beyond your understanding. Write about:

— What helped you maintain your faith during that time?

— Were there any signs or moments that reassured you of the right path?

— How did this experience shape your understanding of trusting God's timing?

4. Obedience and Acceptance:

— Consider the concept of obedience in your life. Reflect on a situation where you felt called to make a difficult decision. Write about:

— What factors influenced your decision to obey or resist?

— How did your understanding of obedience evolve through that experience?

— What did you learn about yourself and your relationship with God?

5. Desire for Change:

— Write about an area in your life where you seek change or fulfillment. Consider:

— What specific changes do you long for, and why are they important to you?

— How does your faith inform your approach to seeking these changes?

— What steps can you take to align your actions with your desires and trust in divine guidance?

6. Discussion Sharing (Optional):

— In a group setting, share one insight from your reflections that resonates with you. This could be a lesson learned about prayer, trust, or obedience, or a personal realization regarding your spiritual journey.

CLOSING:

As you complete this exercise, embrace the journey of prayer and reflection as a means to deepen your relationship with God. Recognize that navigating trust and obedience can be challenging, but these struggles often lead to profound personal growth and clarity. By actively engaging with your feelings and desires, you empower yourself to seek the fulfillment you seek while remaining open to divine guidance. Trust the process, and be patient with yourself as you continue on this path of exploration and transformation.

NOTES

_____

_____

_____

_____

_____

_____

_____

_____

_____

_____

_____

_____

NOTES

NOTES

_____

_____

_____

_____

_____

_____

_____

_____

_____

_____

_____

_____

_____

NOTES

NOTES

UNFORESEEN DEPARTURES: TURMOIL IN MARRIAGE

This chapter centers on the emotional and practical upheavals that follow the husband's sudden departure from the household. The chapter vividly illustrates the chaos and heartache that arise when a partner leaves unexpectedly, disrupting not only the emotional equilibrium but also the financial stability of the family.

CENTRAL THEME: THE PROFOUND IMPACT OF AN ABRUPT MARITAL SEPARATION ON BOTH PERSONAL AND FINANCIAL ASPECTS OF LIFE.

1. **Emotional Turmoil:** The chapter explores the deep emotional pain and confusion experienced by the narrator after her husband's departure. The initial shock of finding him gone, coupled with his removal of personal belongings including her jewelry, underscores the sense of betrayal and loss. The narrator grapples with unanswered questions about his motivations and the abrupt nature of his exit, which leaves her heartbroken and bewildered.

2. **Financial Strain:** Alongside emotional distress, the chapter delves into the financial difficulties that arise from the separation. The narrator's struggle to manage bills alone, her reliance on retirement savings, and her ongoing efforts to seek financial stability highlight the significant financial burden placed on her as a result of her husband's actions. This financial strain is compounded by his secretive behavior regarding finances and his failure to fully support the family.

3. **Communication Breakdown:** The chapter illustrates the breakdown in communication between the narrator and her husband. Despite the narrator's attempts to understand and address the issues in their marriage, her husband's lack of transparency and unwillingness to discuss his dissatisfaction contribute to the collapse of their relationship. His subsequent actions, including the divorce proceedings initiated without her knowledge, further exacerbate the sense of betrayal.

4. **Personal Growth and Resilience:** Despite the challenges, the narrator finds strength and resilience through her faith and personal initiatives. She begins to engage in activities that empower her, such as participating in the Women of Destiny Empowerment Ministry and starting her own coaching business. This personal growth signifies a shift from being overwhelmed by the crisis to taking proactive steps towards rebuilding her life.

5. Legal and Practical Challenges: The chapter concludes with the narrator facing legal and practical challenges related to the divorce process. Her interaction with a lawyer and the daunting task of providing required documents highlight the complexities and emotional strain of navigating a legal separation.

Overall, Chapter 4 captures the multifaceted impact of an unexpected departure on a person's life, encompassing emotional, financial, and practical dimensions. It portrays the narrator's journey through heartbreak and uncertainty, while also showcasing her resilience and determination to rebuild and move forward.

DISCUSSION QUESTIONS

1. Initial Reactions to Unexpected Events:

— The author describes her shock and heartbreak upon finding her husband had packed and left. How do you typically react to unexpected and distressing changes in your life? How do you process and cope with sudden disruptions?

2. Midlife Crisis and Personal Challenges:

— The chapter raises the possibility of a midlife crisis influencing the husband's behavior. What are your thoughts on how midlife crises impact relationships and personal decisions? Have you experienced or witnessed similar challenges in others' lives?

3. Financial Strain and Transparency:

— The author mentions financial strain and secrecy in her marriage. How important is financial transparency in a relationship? How can couples work together to manage finances effectively and honestly?

4. Role of Trust and Communication:

— Trust and communication are central to the author's experience. How do you build and maintain trust in a relationship, especially when faced with issues like secrecy or financial disagreements?

5. Handling Financial Difficulties:

— The author took proactive steps to manage her finances despite the strain. What strategies have you found effective for handling financial difficulties, either personally or in a relationship?

6. Balancing Personal Needs and Marital Duties:

— Despite her husband's departure, the author continued to fulfill her marital duties. How do you balance personal needs with obligations to a partner, especially in challenging circumstances?

7. Seeking Support and Guidance:

— The author relied on prayer and support from her faith. How do you seek and find support when facing personal crises? What role does faith or spiritual practice play in your coping mechanisms?

8. Navigating Emotional and Practical Changes:

— The chapter describes a mix of emotional and practical adjustments following the husband's departure. How do you manage the emotional impact of significant life changes while also addressing practical concerns?

9. Discovering Strength and Independence:

— The author found a renewed sense of strength and purpose through various activities and new opportunities. How do you rediscover your strength and independence after experiencing personal turmoil or upheaval?

10. Impact of Separation on Family Dynamics:

— The author's family dynamics shifted with her husband's departure. How do separations or significant changes in a family affect relationship among other family members? How can families support each other through such transitions?

11. Maintaining Hope and Faith During Trials:

— The author-maintained hope and faith despite her difficulties. How do you keep hope alive during times of trial? What practices or mindsets help you stay optimistic and resilient?

12. Navigating Uncertainty and Change:

— The chapter reflects on dealing with uncertainty about the future. How do you approach and manage uncertainty in your life, whether related to relationships, finances, or other aspects?

13. Influence of External Support Networks:

— The author engaged with a support group and started new ventures. How do external support networks and community involvement help you navigate difficult periods? Have you found similar groups or networks beneficial?

14. Balancing Personal and Family Priorities:

— The author made a point of prioritizing her son's needs despite her marital issues. How do you balance personal challenges with family responsibilities? What strategies help you maintain focus on what matters most?

15. Reflection on Personal Growth Through Adversity:

— Reflecting on the author's journey, how can personal growth emerge from adversity? Share examples of how overcoming challenges has led to personal development in your own life.

These questions aim to stimulate thoughtful discussion about handling personal and relational challenges, maintaining trust and communication, and finding strength and purpose in the face of adversity.

16. Understanding Communication Breakdown:

— The author's husband claimed she no longer loved him and focused on his own feelings and perceptions. How do communication breakdowns affect relationships? What steps can couples take to improve communication and avoid misunderstandings?

17. Impact of Sudden Decisions:

— The husband's decision to leave was abrupt and unilateral. How do sudden decisions in relationships impact both partners? What strategies can help both parties cope with unexpected changes?

18. Handling Emotional Overwhelm:

— The author experienced an overwhelming moment of prayer during the drive. How do you manage overwhelming emotions or spiritual experiences during a crisis? What role does emotional and spiritual support play in your coping process?

19. Evaluating the Role of Trust:

– The author felt deceived and struggled with her husband's secrecy and his abrupt departure. How can trust be rebuilt in a relationship after it has been damaged? What are some ways to address feelings of betrayal?

20. Seeking Counseling:

– The chapter discusses previous attempts at counseling and their outcomes. What are some effective ways to approach counseling or therapy in a relationship? How can partners ensure that counseling is productive?

21. Dealing with Unfulfilled Expectations:

– The author's husband's departure and subsequent actions left her feeling unfulfilled and confused. How do unfulfilled expectations impact one's emotional well-being? How can individuals address and manage these feelings?

22. Role of Personal Growth and Self-Care:

– The husband encouraged the author to focus on her personal growth and happiness. How important is self-care and personal development during times of crisis? What practices have you found effective for personal growth?

23. Understanding Different Perspectives:

– The husband's view of the relationship and the author's perspective were at odds. How can understanding and validating each other's perspectives help resolve conflicts? How do you approach a situation where perspectives are vastly different?

24. Confronting Unresolved Issues:

— The author was left with many unanswered questions after her husband's departure. How do you deal with unresolved issues and questions in a relationship? What approaches can help in finding closure?

25. Impact of External Actions on Personal Feelings:

— The chapter describes the impact of divorce papers and the husband's speech. How do external actions, such as legal proceedings or significant gestures, affect your emotional state? How do you cope with the emotional fallout of such actions?

26. Navigating the End of a Relationship:

— The author struggled with the finality of her husband's decision and the end of their marriage. How do you navigate the process of ending a significant relationship? What steps can help in coping with the end of a long-term relationship?

27. Reflecting on Personal and Relationship Dynamics:

— The author reflects on her role and experiences in the relationship. How important is self-reflection in understanding the dynamics of a relationship? How can reflecting on past experiences inform future relationship choices?

28. Support Systems During Crisis:

— The author found support through prayer and her faith. What role do support systems, whether they are spiritual, familial, or social, play during times of personal crisis? How can you build and utilize a strong support network?

29. Learning from Relationship Challenges:

— The chapter describes various challenges and struggles within the marriage. What lessons can be learned from difficult relationship experiences? How can these lessons be applied to future relationships or personal growth?

30. Balancing Compassion and Self-Respect:

— The author exhibited compassion for her husband while grappling with her own pain and self-respect. How can you balance compassion for others with maintaining self-respect and personal boundaries? What strategies help in managing this balance?

These questions aim to facilitate a deep and reflective discussion about the themes of communication, trust, personal growth, and the impact of significant life changes on relationships.

REFLECTIVE EXERCISE:
NAVIGATING TURMOIL AND EMBRACING RESILIENCE

PURPOSE:

To encourage readers to reflect on their own experiences with loss, change, and resilience, and to identify actionable steps toward healing and empowerment.

INSTRUCTIONS:

1. Journaling Prompt:

— Reflect on a time when you faced an unexpected loss or significant change in your life. Write about the initial emotions you experienced. Consider:

— What feelings surfaced when you encountered this change (e.g., shock, betrayal, confusion)?

— How did this experience impact your emotional well-being in the short and long term?

2. Identifying Financial Strain:

— If applicable, think about a time when financial challenges added to your emotional distress. Write about:

— How did you manage your finances during that period?

— What support systems or resources helped you navigate those challenges?

— What lessons did you learn about financial resilience?

3. Communication Reflection:

— Consider a relationship where communication broke down, leading to misunderstandings or conflict. Write about:

— What were the key factors that contributed to the breakdown in communication?

— How did you attempt to address the issues, and what was the outcome?

— What insights did you gain about the importance of open and honest communication?

4. Personal Growth and Empowerment:

— Reflect on how adversity has prompted personal growth in your life. Write about:

— An initiative or activity you undertook to regain your sense of control or empowerment after a difficult experience.

— How did engaging in this activity contribute to your resilience and personal development?

— What strengths did you discover in yourself during this process?

5. Facing Legal and Practical Challenges:

— If you have faced legal or logistical challenges, consider how you approached them. Write about:

— What steps did you take to navigate these complexities?

— How did you cope with the stress associated with these challenges?

— What resources or support systems were most helpful to you during this time?

6. Setting Intentions for the Future:

— Write a short paragraph outlining one or two actionable steps you can take to move forward positively from your current challenges. Consider:

— What support do you need to seek or reinforce in your life?

— How can you cultivate resilience and hope in your journey ahead?

7. Discussion Sharing (Optional):

— In a group setting, share one key insight from your reflections that resonates with you. This could be about emotional healing, financial management, or personal growth through adversity.

CLOSING:

As you complete this exercise, honor the complexities of navigating loss and upheaval. Recognize that while these experiences can be incredibly challenging, they also offer opportunities for growth and resilience. By reflecting on your feelings and experiences, you empower yourself to take actionable steps toward healing and rebuilding your life. Remember to be patient with yourself as you navigate this journey, and trust that each step brings you closer to a renewed sense of purpose and strength.

NOTES

NOTES

NOTES

NOTES

NOTES

NOTES

5

TRUSTING IN DREAMS: THE PATH TO FORGIVENESS

CENTRAL THEME: FORGIVENESS AMIDST PERSONAL TRIALS AND DIVINE GUIDANCE.

1. **Navigating Personal Struggles:** The chapter opens with the author's difficult experience of dealing with a legal separation and the subsequent financial and emotional challenges. The author grapples with feelings of betrayal and frustration as her husband fails to fulfill his responsibilities and engages in reckless behavior.

2. Spiritual Reflection and Prayer: Amidst these struggles, the author turns to prayer and fasting, seeking divine guidance and protection for her estranged husband. This period of intense spiritual reflection leads to a series of vivid and prophetic dreams, which she interprets as messages from God.

3. Dreams as Divine Communication: The author describes how her dreams become a significant means through which she receives divine messages. These dreams often contain warnings and encouragements, prompting her to remain vigilant and hopeful despite her circumstances.

4. Forgiveness and Reconciliation: A central part of the chapter is the author's journey toward forgiveness. Despite her husband's shortcomings and the pain he has caused, she feels compelled by God to forgive him. This is demonstrated through her public declaration of forgiveness during a radio interview and a heartfelt apology when he visits her home. The chapter underscores the transformative power of forgiveness, both for the person extending it and for the one receiving it.

5. Divine Assurance and New Beginnings: The chapter concludes with the author reflecting on how her dreams and divine messages assure her of a new season in her life. She feels that God is guiding her toward personal growth and renewal, promising that despite the trials, there is hope and a brighter future ahead.

In essence, the chapter emphasizes how faith and forgiveness can guide individuals through the most challenging times, highlighting the importance of divine guidance and personal growth in overcoming adversity.

DISCUSSION QUESTIONS

1. Handling Legal and Emotional Challenges:

— How did the author navigate the complexities of legal separation while managing emotional pain? What strategies can individuals use to cope with similar challenges in their own lives?

2. Impact on Children:

— The author observed the impact of her husband's inconsistent presence on their children. How can parents ensure that their children are supported emotionally during a separation or divorce? What are effective ways to manage disappointment and maintain stability for children?

3. Financial Strain and Boundaries:

— The author faced financial strain due to her husband's requests for money. How can individuals set and maintain financial boundaries during a separation or divorce? What are the best practices for managing financial responsibilities and avoiding exploitation?

4. Role of Generosity:

— The author felt that her act of generosity became a precedent for further demands. How can individuals balance generosity with self-preservation in relationships? What are the signs that generosity might be taken advantage of?

5. Praying for Others:

– The author continued to pray for her husband despite their separation. What role does prayer or spiritual practice play in coping with marital difficulties? How can it be a source of strength or guidance?

6. Interpreting Dreams:

– The author had vivid dreams that she interpreted as messages from God. How can dreams and other spiritual experiences provide insight during challenging times? What are some ways to discern and interpret such messages?

7. Dealing with Reckless Behavior:

– The author was troubled by her husband's reckless behavior, such as allowing their son to drive with expired tags. How should one address concerns about unsafe or irresponsible behavior by an ex-partner, especially when it impacts children?

8. Navigating Communication with an Ex-Partner:

– The author faced difficulties in communicating effectively with her husband regarding legal and financial matters. What are effective communication strategies when dealing with an ex-partner, especially in contentious situations?

9. Finding Support and Resources:

– The author sought legal assistance and support from a church member. How can individuals find and utilize support resources during a legal separation or divorce? What role can community and faith-based support play?

10. Understanding and Managing Anxiety:

— The author experienced anxiety related to her legal and financial situation. What are effective methods for managing anxiety and stress during major life changes? How can one maintain emotional well-being in the face of uncertainty?

11. Addressing Rumors and Speculation:

— The author dealt with rumors about her husband's activities. How can individuals handle rumors and speculation during a separation or divorce? What is the best approach to address and confront unverified information?

12. Reflection and Personal Growth:

— The author reflected on her experiences through dreams and divine guidance. How can reflection and personal insights contribute to healing and growth during difficult times? What role does self-awareness play in overcoming challenges?

13. Balancing Hope and Reality:

— The author hoped for a change while dealing with the reality of her situation. How can individuals balance hope for resolution or reconciliation with acceptance of the current circumstances? What strategies help in moving forward with hope and realism?

14. Empowerment through Faith:

— The author's faith played a significant role in her journey. How can faith or spirituality empower individuals to face and overcome personal struggles? What practices or beliefs contribute to resilience and strength?

15. Support Systems and Emotional Resilience:

– The author had to build a support system to handle her legal and emotional struggles. How important is having a support network during times of crisis? What types of support are most beneficial for building emotional resilience?

These questions are designed to facilitate deep reflection and discussion about managing the challenges described in the text, while also exploring broader themes of support, personal growth, and emotional well-being.

For the section of Chapter 5 that focuses on forgiveness, divine communication, and personal transformation, here are some small group discussion questions:

16. Understanding Divine Guidance:

– How did the author discern God's call to talk about forgiveness during her radio interview? How can we differentiate between divine guidance and personal desires when making decisions?

17. The Role of Forgiveness:

– The author was directed by God to publicly forgive her husband. What challenges might someone face when forgiving someone who has wronged them deeply? How can forgiveness impact both the forgiver and the forgiven?

18. Public and Private Forgiveness:

– The author shared her need to forgive publicly on the radio and personally with her husband. What are the differences between public and private forgiveness? How can both forms of forgiveness play a role in healing relationships?

19. Emotional Expression and Prayer:

– The author experienced a powerful emotional response during her prayer for her husband. How can prayer and emotional expression help in processing feelings of hurt and forgiveness? What are some ways to manage emotions while offering forgiveness?

20. Impact of Past Memories:

– The author reflected on joyful memories of her marriage. How can reflecting on positive memories help in the process of forgiveness and healing? What role do positive memories play in overcoming current challenges?

21. Role of Dreams in Spiritual Guidance:

– The author received what she believed to be prophetic dreams during this period. How can dreams or other spiritual experiences contribute to understanding and navigating personal challenges? What is the best approach to interpreting these experiences?

22. Transitioning to a New Season:

– The author's dream symbolized a transition from the old to the new. How can individuals embrace new beginnings while dealing with past pain? What strategies can help in moving forward during significant life changes?

23. Role of Faith in Forgiveness:

– The author's faith played a crucial role in her ability to forgive and move forward. How does faith or spirituality influence one's capacity to forgive and seek personal growth? What practices can strengthen this faith?

24. Challenges of Self-Forgiveness:

– The author discussed the difficulty of forgiving oneself. What are some common barriers to self-forgiveness? How can individuals work towards self-forgiveness, especially when their actions have impacted others?

25. Handling Unexpected Reactions:

– The author's husband seemed bewildered by her actions and forgiveness. How should one approach situations where the other party does not respond as expected to acts of forgiveness? What can be done when forgiveness is met with confusion or resistance?

26. Navigating Emotional Overwhelm:

– The author experienced emotional overwhelm during her interactions with her husband. How can individuals cope with and manage overwhelming emotions during difficult personal interactions? What are some techniques for maintaining composure and clarity?

27. Significance of Divine Messages:

– The author felt that the voice and dreams she experienced were messages from God. How can one discern and respond to what they believe to be divine messages? What role do personal beliefs and experiences play in interpreting such messages?

28. Support Systems in Difficult Times:

– The author had a support system that included spiritual guidance and personal reflections. How important is it to have a support system during times of personal crisis? What types of support are most beneficial?

29. Practical Steps Towards Reconciliation:

– The author took several practical steps towards reconciliation, including public and private expressions of forgiveness. What practical steps can individuals take to move towards reconciliation in their own relationships? How can these steps be adapted to different situations?

30. Balancing Reflection and Action:

– The author reflected on past memories while taking action towards forgiveness and personal growth. How can one balance reflection on past experiences with taking proactive steps towards healing and improvement? What is the role of reflection in personal development?

These questions are intended to facilitate a meaningful discussion on the themes of forgiveness, personal transformation, and the role of spiritual guidance in overcoming challenges.

REFLECTIVE EXERCISE:
EXPLORING FORGIVENESS AND DIVINE GUIDANCE

PURPOSE:

To encourage readers to reflect on their own paths to forgiveness, consider the role of spiritual guidance in their lives, and identify actionable steps toward healing.

INSTRUCTIONS:

1. Journaling Prompt:

— Reflect on a situation where you felt betrayed or hurt by someone you cared about. Write about:

— The emotions you experienced during that time (e.g., anger, sadness, confusion).

— How this betrayal affected your relationship with that person and your overall well-being.

2. The Role of Prayer and Reflection:

— Consider times when you turned to prayer or spiritual practices for comfort and guidance. Write about:

— What prompted you to seek spiritual support during that time?

— How did prayer or reflection help you navigate your emotions or circumstances?

— Did you experience any moments of clarity or insight during this process?

3. Dreams and Divine Messages:

— If you have ever experienced significant dreams that felt meaningful, reflect on those experiences. Write about:

— A dream that resonated with you and what you believe it communicated.

— How did this dream impact your feelings or decisions regarding your situation?

— What do you think the role of intuition or subconscious messages is in guiding your path?

4. The Journey to Forgiveness:

— Write about your personal views on forgiveness. Reflect on:

— What forgiveness means to you, and what challenges you face in forgiving others.

— An experience where you offered or received forgiveness. How did it transform the relationship or your emotions?

— What steps can you take to move toward forgiveness in a current situation?

5. Finding Assurance and New Beginnings:

— Think about a time when you felt a sense of hope or new beginnings after a difficult period. Write about:

— What signs or experiences reassured you that a positive change was coming?

— How can you cultivate hope in your current circumstances?

— What new beginnings or personal growth are you open to exploring in your life?

6. Setting Intentions for Healing:

— Write a short paragraph outlining one or two actionable steps you can take toward forgiveness or personal growth. Consider:

— How can you actively practice forgiveness in your daily life?

— What support systems or resources can you seek to help you along this journey?

7. Discussion Sharing (Optional):

— In a group setting, share one insight from your reflections that resonates with you. This could be about your understanding of forgiveness, the role of prayer, or the importance of divine guidance in your life.

CLOSING:

As you complete this exercise, recognize that the journey to forgiveness and healing is deeply personal and often complex. Embrace the insights you've gained and consider how faith and reflection can guide you through challenging times. By taking intentional steps toward forgiveness and growth, you empower yourself to create a brighter future filled with hope and renewal. Remember, each small step can lead to profound transformation in your life.

NOTES

NOTES

NOTES

NOTES

NOTES

TURMOIL AND TRIALS: THE UNRAVELING OF TRUTH

6

Central Theme of Chapter 6 is divine intervention and miraculous provision during times of uncertainty and trial. This theme is developed through the following elements:

1. **Discovery and Uncertainty:** The chapter opens with a sense of growing unease as the author discovers a parking pass for an unfamiliar location in her husband's car. This discovery leads to suspicions about his true activities and circumstances, amplifying her feelings of doubt and anxiety.

2. **Faith and Prophetic Assurance:** Despite the mounting concerns, the author maintains her faith through prayer and seeking spiritual guidance. A prophetic prayer call reassures

her with promises of miraculous provision and financial blessings, offering a sense of hope and direction.

3. **Miraculous Provision:** The author's decision to act on faith—applying for a car loan despite her poor credit—leads to an unexpected and favorable outcome at the dealership. The discrepancy between her credit score and the interest rate she receives is perceived as a sign of divine intervention, reinforcing her faith in God's promises.

4. **Joy and Gratitude:** The author's celebration of the new car, which she sees as a tangible manifestation of divine provision. This moment of joy and gratitude symbolizes a positive shift in her circumstances and underscores the theme of miraculous support in challenging times.

In Part 2 of Chapter 6, the theme transitions to spiritual reassurance and divine promise amidst personal and relational turmoil:

1. **Family and Rumors:** The author's trip to South Carolina with her family provides temporary solace, but it is overshadowed by distressing rumors about her husband. This adds another layer of emotional strain and uncertainty to her situation.

2. **Interactions with Her Husband:** A tense encounter with her husband, coupled with his unexplained behavior, further complicates her emotional state. The author chooses to remain silent and rely on spiritual guidance, feeling led by the Holy Spirit to avoid confrontation.

3. **Dream and Divine Message:** A dream and a subsequent divine message offer reassurance and guidance, emphasizing that her prayers are being answered and that she is entering a period of blessings and divine favor. This message provides comfort and encourages her to trust in God's plan.

4. **Divine Assurance and Harvest**: The divine message underscores a forthcoming "harvest" of blessings, emphasizing that she should not be consumed by worries about her husband or finances. Instead, she is encouraged to focus on her spiritual journey and trust in divine intervention.

Overall, the chapter illustrates how faith, prayer, and divine intervention intersect to provide miraculous support and reassurance during periods of uncertainty and trial. The narrative highlights the power of spiritual belief and trust in divine promises as a source of strength and hope amidst personal challenges.

DISCUSSION QUESTIONS

1. Initial Reactions:

— How did the discovery of the parking pass affect the author's trust in her husband? What are some ways that unexpected findings can impact relationships and trust?

2. Balancing Practical Needs and Spiritual Faith:

— The author prayed for protection and guidance while dealing with practical needs, such as acquiring a new vehicle. How can one balance practical concerns with spiritual faith in everyday life?

3. Influence of Prophetic Messages:

— The author received a prophetic message about blessings and financial increase. How do prophetic messages influence our faith and decisions? How should one discern and act upon such messages?

4. Experience of Divine Intervention:

— The author felt a sense of divine intervention when acquiring a new car. How do personal experiences of what one perceives as divine intervention affect our faith and actions? Have you experienced something similar?

5. Emotional Responses to Miraculous Outcomes:

– The author felt overwhelming gratitude and emotion when her financial situation changed unexpectedly. How do you handle and process intense emotions in the face of unexpected positive outcomes?

6. Handling Gossip and Rumors:

– The author overheard rumors about her husband during a family visit. How should one approach handling and responding to gossip or rumors, especially when they concern personal matters?

7. Role of Faith in Times of Trial:

– The author leaned heavily on faith during a period of personal turmoil. How can faith provide support and guidance during times of personal or family crises?

8. Impact of Family and Support Systems:

– The author's trip to South Carolina with her family brought her joy and comfort. How important is a support system or community during times of trial? What role can family and friends play in supporting us?

9. Dealing with Financial and Practical Challenges:

– The author faced financial challenges and managed to secure a new vehicle despite an unfavorable credit score. What practical steps can be taken to manage financial stress and challenges? How can faith and prayer complement these efforts?

10. Discernment and Trust:

– The author had to discern the truth behind the rumors and her husband's actions. How can one effectively discern the truth in complex situations involving relationships and external opinions?

11. Spiritual Growth and Personal Gifts:

– The prophetic message mentioned gifts and a call to use them. How can individuals recognize and cultivate their personal gifts and talents, especially during times of trial and uncertainty?

12. Faith and Unanswered Questions:

– The author had unanswered questions about her husband's actions and the rumors she heard. How can one maintain faith and peace when faced with unanswered questions or unresolved issues?

13. Experiencing and Recognizing Divine Provision:

– The author recognized what she perceived as divine provision in the acquisition of the car. How can one recognize and appreciate moments of divine provision in their own life?

14. Managing Conflicting Information:

– The author dealt with conflicting information about her husband's lifestyle and the prophetic message she received. How can one manage and navigate conflicting information or advice in their personal life?

15. Planning and Decision-Making:

— The author made plans to visit family and manage the new car. How do you approach planning and decision-making during times of personal or family upheaval? What factors should be considered?

These questions aim to encourage discussion about the intersection of faith, personal challenges, and the ways in which divine intervention and prophetic messages impact our lives.

16. Handling Disappointments:

— How did the author's husband's actions (not showing up as promised) impact her emotionally and spiritually? How do you handle disappointment or unmet expectations in your own life?

17. Responding to Unexpected Generosity:

— The husband brought a new cell phone for their youngest son. How do you perceive this gesture in the context of the family's situation? How can we differentiate between genuine acts of kindness and gestures that might have other motives?

18. Listening to Inner Promptings:

— The author mentions that the Holy Spirit silenced her when she was about to speak. How do you discern between your own thoughts and the guidance of the Holy Spirit? How important is it to listen to these inner promptings in difficult situations?

19. Interpreting Dreams:

– The author had a dream involving pills and a meeting about increasing property values. What might these elements symbolize in the context of her situation? How do you interpret dreams or symbolic messages in your own life?

20. Faith and Assurance:

– The author received a message from God assuring her of His presence and promises. How does receiving such divine reassurance impact your faith and daily life? How do you stay encouraged when faced with uncertainty?

21. Trusting in Divine Timing:

– The message talks about a harvest time and promises of blessings. How do you understand and trust in divine timing and promises when they seem delayed or when facing immediate challenges?

22. Letting Go of Control:

– God instructed the author to stop trying to fix her husband and let Him take care of him. How do you find it challenging to let go of control in situations where you feel responsible for others' well-being? How can faith help you in releasing control?

23. Prayers and Intercession:

– The author was encouraged to continue praying and interceding. How do you maintain a prayerful and intercessory attitude even when answers to prayers seem slow in coming?

24. Experiencing Harvest and Blessings:

– The message mentions a time of harvest and blessings. How do you recognize and prepare for seasons of blessing in your own life? What steps can you take to remain open to receiving blessings?

25. Dealing with Emotional and Spiritual Wounds:

– The message also talks about healing and being ushered into new things. How can one process and heal from emotional and spiritual wounds while awaiting new blessings and opportunities?

26. Role of Community and Support:

– How important is community support and prayer from others when facing personal trials? How can you offer support to others who might be going through similar situations?

27. Balancing Hope and Reality:

– How do you balance holding on to hope and divine promises with dealing with the practical realities of challenging situations?

28. Understanding Divine Intervention:

– The author received assurances of divine intervention and support. How do you understand and experience divine intervention in your life? What signs or outcomes confirm this for you?

29. Managing Uncertainty:

— How do you manage feelings of uncertainty and anxiety while waiting for divine promises or answers to prayers?

30. Personal Reflection on the Promises of God:

— Reflect on the promises and assurances given in the message. How do you integrate these promises into your personal life and faith journey?

These questions aim to encourage reflection on personal faith, spiritual guidance, and practical responses to life's challenges.

REFLECTIVE EXERCISE: EMBRACING FAITH AMIDST UNCERTAINTY

PURPOSE:

To encourage readers to reflect on their own experiences with uncertainty, faith, and the presence of divine support in their lives.

INSTRUCTIONS:

1. Journaling Prompt:

— Reflect on a time when you faced uncertainty or doubt in your life. Write about:

— What specific situation caused you to feel uneasy or anxious?

— How did this uncertainty affect your emotions and decision-making?

2. Seeking Spiritual Guidance:

— Consider instances when you turned to prayer or spiritual practices for clarity and re-assurance. Write about:

— What prompted you to seek divine guidance?

— How did you feel during this process, and what insights or comfort did you receive?

3. Recognizing Miraculous Provision:

– Reflect on moments when you experienced unexpected support or blessings during challenging times. Write about:

– A specific instance where you felt something positive happen that seemed beyond your control.

– How did this experience reinforce your faith or change your perspective?

4. Joy and Gratitude:

– Think about how you celebrate moments of joy and gratitude in your life, especially after difficult periods. Write about:

– What does it mean for you to acknowledge and celebrate blessings?

– How can practicing gratitude shift your focus from anxiety to appreciation?

5. Navigating Relationship Challenges:

– Reflect on a difficult interaction with someone close to you. Write about:

– How did you approach the situation, and what emotions did you experience?

– Did you choose to respond differently than you normally would? If so, what guided that decision?

6. Dreams and Divine Messages:

– If you've had dreams or insights that felt meaningful or prophetic, reflect on those experiences. Write about:

— A dream that provided guidance or reassurance. What was the message, and how did it impact your actions or thoughts?

— How do you interpret signs or messages in your life, and how do they influence your faith journey?

7. Setting Intentions for Trust:

— Write a short paragraph outlining one or two actionable steps you can take to cultivate trust in divine guidance in your life. Consider:

— How can you strengthen your spiritual practices or increase your awareness of divine support?

— What fears or anxieties can you consciously release to create space for trust and hope?

8. Discussion Sharing (Optional):

— In a group setting, share one key insight from your reflections that resonates with you. This could be about faith, the power of prayer, or recognizing divine support in your life.

CLOSING:

As you complete this exercise, recognize the profound impact of faith and spiritual reflection in navigating uncertainty. Embrace the insights you've gained and consider how divine guidance can serve as a source of strength in challenging times. By intentionally focusing on trust, gratitude, and spiritual growth, you can foster a deeper sense of peace and resilience as you journey through life's trials. Remember, each moment of faith strengthens your ability to navigate the complexities of your path.

NOTES

NOTES

NOTES

NOTES

NOTES

NOTES

PART II

THE FAMILY FAÇADE-NAVIGATING THE WEBS OF BETRAYAL WOVEN BY NARCISSISTIC ABUSE

The overall theme of Part II is the pervasive and enduring impact of narcissistic abuse and the multifaceted ways in which it continues through the actions of the narcissist's family.

This section examines how narcissistic abuse extends beyond the direct actions of the narcissist, revealing how their family members perpetuate and exacerbate the victim's suffering. Here's a breakdown of how this theme is developed:

1. **Narcissistic Manipulation and Deception**: The theme begins with an exploration of how narcissists skillfully manipulate their environment, projecting a false image while distorting the truth about their victims. This manipulation creates a misleading narrative that garners sympathy for the narcissist and alienates the true victim, setting the stage for ongoing abuse.

2. **Posthumous Manipulation**: The theme extends to the aftermath of the narcissist's death, showing how their family members may continue to perpetuate deceit to protect the deceased's image. This ongoing manipulation involves spreading misinformation and malicious gossip to discredit the victim and obscure the nature of the abuse, further complicating the victim's path to justice and healing.

3. **Forms of Abuse by Family Members**: The section delves into various forms of abuse inflicted by the narcissist's family, including:

- Emotional Betrayal: Family members undermine the victim's emotional well-being through deceit and manipulation.

- Social Isolation: Victims are cut off from support networks and social connections due to harmful misinformation spread by family members.

— Mental Manipulation: Psychological tactics are used to destabilize the victim's mental health and sense of reality.

— Identity Theft: Family members engage in or facilitate the theft and misuse of the victim's identity, adding further complexity to their recovery.

4. **Complex Recovery and Justice**: The theme highlights how these forms of abuse and manipulation make the victim's journey toward recovery and justice significantly more challenging. The persistence of these harmful behaviors by the narcissist's family members complicates the victim's efforts to heal and reclaim their life.

Overall, Part II emphasizes the broader and more insidious effects of narcissistic abuse, illustrating how the impact of the abuse extends beyond the narcissist to include their family, who continue to perpetuate harm through various means. This section underscores the complexity of the victim's experience and the need for recognition and understanding of the pervasive nature of narcissistic abuse.

DISCUSSION QUESTIONS

1. Understanding Narcissistic Abuse:

— How do you perceive the impact of narcissistic abuse on both the immediate victim and those around them? What are some signs that someone might be experiencing narcissistic abuse?

2. Recognizing Manipulation Tactics:

— The text describes narcissists as adept at charming and deceiving others while fabricating falsehoods. Can you share any personal experiences or observations where manipulation by a narcissistic person created a false narrative? How did it affect relationships?

3. Family Dynamics:

— In what ways do you think family members might perpetuate the narcissist's abuse even after their death? How might this continuation of abuse manifest in various forms, such as gossip or neglect?

4. Emotional Betrayal:

— The text discusses emotional betrayal by the narcissist's family. What are some examples of how emotional betrayal can undermine a victim's stability? How can victims recognize and address these forms of betrayal?

5. Social Isolation:

— How do family members contribute to the victim's social isolation? Have you encountered or heard of situations where someone was cut off from their support network due to the influence of a narcissist or their family?

6. Financial Exploitation:

— Financial exploitation is one of the abuses mentioned. What are some ways in which a narcissist or their family might misuse or control someone's financial resources? How can victims protect themselves from such exploitation?

7. Mental Manipulation:

— The text refers to psychological tactics used to destabilize the victim's mental health. What are some common psychological tactics used in narcissistic abuse, and how can individuals recognize and counteract them?

8. Identity Theft:

— Identity theft is highlighted as a form of abuse. In what ways can family members facilitate or engage in identity theft? How can victims work to reclaim and protect their personal identity?

9. Navigating Recovery:

— Given the complexity of dealing with both direct and indirect abuse from a narcissist and their family, what are some effective strategies for recovery and healing? How can victims seek justice and recognition despite ongoing deceit?

10. Support Systems:

– What role do support systems play in helping victims of narcissistic abuse? How can friends, family, and professionals effectively support someone dealing with these issues?

11. Identifying and Confronting Deception:

– How can individuals identify when they are being deceived or manipulated by a narcissist or their family members? What steps can be taken to confront or address these deceptions?

12. Personal Boundaries:

– How important are personal boundaries in dealing with narcissistic abuse? What strategies can individuals use to maintain healthy boundaries while navigating complex family dynamics?

13. Impact of False Narratives:

– How do false narratives created by narcissists and their families impact the victim's reputation and relationships? What can victims do to counteract or dispel these falsehoods?

14. Legal and Financial Protection:

– What legal and financial measures can individuals take to protect themselves from exploitation and identity theft? Are there resources or organizations that can provide assistance?

15. Self-Care and Healing:

— How can victims prioritize self-care and healing amidst the ongoing effects of narcissistic abuse? What practices or support mechanisms can help in the recovery process?

These questions are meant to encourage discussion, provide support, and offer insights into the multifaceted nature of narcissistic abuse and its impact on individuals and their families.

REFLECTIVE EXERCISE:
UNTANGLING THE WEB OF BETRAYAL

PURPOSE:

To encourage readers to reflect on the complexities of narcissistic abuse, recognize its manifestations in family dynamics, and explore personal pathways to healing and empowerment.

INSTRUCTIONS:

1. Journaling Prompt:

— Reflect on your own experiences with betrayal, whether from a partner or family members. Write about:

— A specific instance of manipulation or deceit that impacted you. How did it make you feel?

— What was the immediate effect on your emotional and mental well-being?

2. Recognizing Manipulation:

— Consider the ways in which manipulation has shown up in your relationships. Write about:

— Instances where someone distorted the truth or created a false narrative. How did that affect your perception of yourself and your reality?

— What signs did you notice that indicated manipulation was occurring?

3. The Role of Family:

— Reflect on how family dynamics have influenced your experiences of abuse. Write about:

— Any family members who perpetuated or ignored the abuse. How did their actions impact your healing journey?

— Feelings of isolation or support (or lack thereof) from family during difficult times. How did that affect your recovery?

4. Forms of Abuse:

— Think about the various forms of abuse discussed in this section. Write about:

— Which form of abuse (emotional betrayal, social isolation, mental manipulation, identity theft) resonated most with your experiences?

— How did this form of abuse manifest in your life, and what strategies did you use to cope?

5. Pathways to Recovery:

— Reflect on your journey toward healing and justice. Write about:

— Steps you've taken to reclaim your identity and well-being. What has been most effective for you?

— Any support systems or resources (friends, therapy, support groups) that have been instrumental in your recovery.

6. Affirming Your Narrative:

– Write a brief personal statement affirming your truth. Consider:

– How can you assert your experiences and emotions despite the manipulations of others?

– What empowering beliefs can you cultivate to support your healing journey?

7. Setting Intentions:

– Write a short paragraph outlining one or two actionable steps you can take to continue your healing process. Consider:

– How can you establish boundaries with those who perpetuate harmful behaviors?

– What practices can you adopt to reinforce your self-worth and resilience?

8. Discussion Sharing (Optional):

– In a group setting, share one key insight from your reflections that stands out to you. This could relate to understanding manipulation, the impact of family, or your path to healing.

CLOSING:

As you complete this exercise, recognize the complex dynamics of narcissistic abuse and the far-reaching effects it can have on individuals and families. Embrace the insights you've gained about your experiences, and consider how acknowledging these truths can empower your journey toward healing. By taking intentional steps to reclaim your narrative and establish healthy boundaries, you create a stronger foundation for your future. Remember, the path to recovery is personal, and each step you take is significant in unraveling the webs of betrayal.

NOTES

NOTES

NOTES

NOTES

NOTES

THE FRACTURED TRUTH: A WEB OF DECEPTION AND GRIEF

This chapter explores the intense emotional turmoil and complex aftermath following the sudden death of the protagonist's husband, emphasizing the profound impact of grief compounded by betrayal and deception.

KEY THEMES AND ELEMENTS OF CHAPTER 7

1. **Sudden and Devastating Loss:** The chapter begins with the protagonist receiving the shocking news of her husband's death, detailing the profound grief and disorientation experienced. The initial shock is so overwhelming that it disrupts the protagonist's ability to think clearly or communicate effectively.

2. **Seeking Answers and Confronting Reality**: In the aftermath, the protagonist seeks answers from authorities, only to be met with a surreal and disheartening reality. The investigation reveals husband's death as potentially caused by natural health issues, but the protagonist is left with lingering questions and a deep sense of disbelief.

3. **Betrayal and Hostility from Family**: The chapter delves into the betrayal and hostility faced from the protagonist's in-laws. The protagonist is subjected to baseless accusations and malicious rumors, which are amplified by family members who seem more interested in tarnishing her reputation than supporting her through grief.

4. **Confronting Deception and Infidelity**: As the chapter progresses, the protagonist uncovers disturbing revelations about her husband's double life, including a long-term relationship with another woman. This discovery deepens the protagonist's sense of betrayal and confusion, as she grapples with the realization that her husband was not the person she thought she knew.

5. **Navigating the Practicalities of Death**: The chapter also covers the logistical challenges of arranging the protagonist husband's funeral and dealing with financial constraints. The protagonist must navigate bureaucratic hurdles, manage funeral arrangements, and seek financial assistance, all while grappling with the emotional weight of her loss.

6. **Isolation and Emotional Struggle**: Throughout the chapter, the protagonist experiences intense feelings of isolation and emotional struggle. The relentless rumors, accusations, and the complexity of dealing with her husband's family leave her feeling abandoned and misunderstood. The protagonist's journey through this chapter highlights her resilience and determination to seek the truth and honor her husband's memory despite overwhelming adversity.

In summary, Chapter 7 illustrates the protagonist's journey through a harrowing period marked by sudden loss, betrayal, and the painful process of uncovering hidden truths. The chapter emphasizes the emotional and practical challenges faced by the protagonist as she navigates a world filled with deception and hostility, all while trying to find closure and manage the aftermath of her husband's death.

DISCUSSION QUESTIONS

1. Immediate Reactions to Loss:

– How did the sudden death of the author's husband affect the narrator emotionally and practically? What are some common emotional and practical challenges people face when dealing with unexpected loss?

2. Dealing with Grief:

– What are some healthy ways to cope with overwhelming grief? How can individuals support themselves and others in the aftermath of a sudden loss?

3. Communication with Authorities:

– How did the interaction with the authorities impact the narrator's sense of closure and understanding of the situation? What role do authorities play in providing clarity and support after a loved one's passing?

4. Handling Unanswered Questions:

– The narrator grapples with unanswered questions about the nature of her husband's death and their relationship. How can individuals find peace or closure when they have unresolved questions about a loved one's passing?

5. Family Dynamics During Grief:

— How did the dynamics within the husband's family affect the narrator's experience of grief and loss? In what ways can family relationships become strained or complicated during times of crisis?

6. False Accusations and Rumors:

— The narrator faced false accusations and rumors from her husband's family. How can someone deal with false accusations while managing their own grief? What strategies might help in maintaining one's integrity amidst such challenges?

7. Impact of Gossip and Rumors:

— How do rumors and gossip affect individuals who are already dealing with personal loss? What can be done to counteract the negative effects of such misinformation?

8. Support Systems:

— The narrator received support from relatives and friends during this difficult time. What qualities make someone a supportive presence during a crisis? How can one offer meaningful support to someone who is grieving?

9. Navigating Relationships:

— How can strained relationships be navigated when dealing with a family member's death? What steps can be taken to address unresolved tensions or grievances in a compassionate manner?

10. Facing Betrayal:

– The narrator experienced feelings of betrayal from the husband's family. How can individuals cope with betrayal from those they once trusted, especially during a time of grief?

11. Confronting Injustice:

– What are some ways to confront and address feelings of injustice and unfair treatment while processing grief? How can one advocate for themselves in the face of false allegations?

12. Trust and Healing:

– How can someone begin to rebuild trust and find healing after being the target of a smear campaign? What steps can be taken to regain a sense of security and well-being?

13. The Role of Faith and Belief:

– How did the narrator's faith influence their ability to cope with grief and betrayal? What role can faith or personal beliefs play in navigating complex emotional challenges?

14. Resilience and Recovery:

– The narrator expresses a desire to face challenges with courage and resilience. What are some strategies for fostering resilience during difficult times? How can individuals stay hopeful despite overwhelming adversity?

15. Personal Reflection:

— Reflecting on the narrator's experience, what insights or lessons can be drawn about dealing with loss, betrayal, and the complexities of familial relationships? How can these lessons be applied to support others facing similar challenges?

These questions are intended to facilitate deep and empathetic discussion, allowing participants to explore the emotional complexities and challenges presented in the text.

16. Dealing with Hostility:

— How did the narrator attempt to handle the hostility and suspicion from her husband's family? What are some strategies for managing and responding to hostility from family members during a time of grief?

17. Conflict Resolution:

— The narrator attempted to reconcile and cooperate with her husband's family but faced resistance. What are some effective methods for resolving conflicts in high-stress situations, especially when emotions are running high?

18. Handling Unexpected Situations:

— The arrival of the sheriff and the discovery of the unknown woman who had been calling about her husband were significant shocks for the narrator. How can individuals prepare for and cope with unexpected and distressing situations that arise during a crisis?

19. Addressing Betrayal:

– How did the narrator process her feelings of betrayal and deceit upon discovering her husband's hidden relationship? What are some healthy ways to address and cope with feelings of betrayal?

20. The Role of Communication:

– The narrator experienced issues with communication both with her husband's family and the authorities. How important is clear and direct communication in handling family disputes and legal matters? What steps can be taken to ensure effective communication?

21. Managing Financial Stress:

– The narrator faced financial challenges related to the funeral expenses. How can one manage financial stress during a crisis, and what resources or strategies can be used to address unexpected financial burdens?

22. Support Systems:

– Despite the challenges, the narrator received support from friends and family. How can a strong support system assist in navigating complex situations, and what qualities make for effective support during times of crisis?

23. Decision-Making During Grief:

– How did the narrator navigate making decisions related to funeral arrangements and handling her husband's belongings? What are some best practices for making important decisions while grieving?

24. Impact of Deception:

— The narrator felt disillusioned by the actions of her husband and his family. How can one come to terms with the impact of deception on their personal relationships and sense of self?

25. Understanding and Forgiveness:

— How did the narrator's faith play a role in her coping process, and how might faith or personal beliefs influence one's ability to understand and forgive in difficult situations?

26. Processing Grief and Anger:

— The narrator experienced intense grief and anger following the events. What are some ways to process and express these emotions constructively? How can individuals find healthy outlets for their grief and anger?

These questions are designed to prompt thoughtful reflection and discussion about the complex emotional and practical challenges faced by the narrator. They encourage exploration of coping mechanisms, conflict resolution, and the impact of grief on personal and familial relationships.

REFLECTIVE EXERCISE:
NAVIGATING GRIEF, BETRAYAL, AND TRUTH

PURPOSE:

This exercise encourages readers to explore their own experiences with grief, betrayal, and the complexities of navigating loss, while reflecting on personal resilience and growth.

INSTRUCTIONS:

1. Journaling Prompt:

— Reflect on a significant loss you've experienced. Write about:

— Your immediate feelings upon receiving the news. What emotions surfaced?

— How did this loss disrupt your daily life or sense of stability?

2. Seeking Answers:

— Consider a time when you sought answers after a loss or betrayal. Write about:

— The questions you had and the challenges you faced in finding clarity.

— How did your search for answers affect your emotional state?

3. Betrayal and Relationships:

— Reflect on any feelings of betrayal you encountered during your grieving process. Write about:

— Specific instances where you felt unsupported or falsely accused by others.

— How did these experiences shape your understanding of trust and relationships?

4. Confronting Hidden Truths:

— Think about any hidden truths you discovered after a significant event. Write about:

— How these revelations impacted your perception of the person or situation.

— The emotional struggle of reconciling the truth with your prior beliefs.

5. Navigating Practicalities:

— Consider the logistical aspects of dealing with loss. Write about:

— Any challenges you faced in managing practical matters (e.g., arrangements, finances) during your grief.

— How you coped with these additional burdens while also processing your emotions.

6. Experiencing Isolation:

— Reflect on moments of feeling isolated during your grieving process. Write about:

— The sources of your isolation (e.g., family dynamics, societal expectations).

— How you found ways to connect with others or nurture your own emotional needs.

7. Resilience and Growth:

— Identify moments of resilience in your journey. Write about:

- How you demonstrated strength despite adversity. What helped you persevere?

- Any lessons learned or insights gained from navigating your experiences.

8. Affirming Your Journey:

- Write a personal statement affirming your right to grieve and heal. Consider:

- What do you want to acknowledge about your grief journey?

- How can you honor your experiences while embracing the path forward?

9. Setting Intentions:

- Conclude by outlining one or two actionable steps you can take to support your healing process. Consider:

- How can you create space for your emotions and seek support when needed?

- What practices or activities can you engage in to foster resilience and well-being?

CLOSING:

As you reflect on these themes, recognize the complexity of grief intertwined with betrayal and deception. Embrace the insights gained about your experiences and allow them to inform your healing journey. Acknowledge your resilience and the strength you possess to navigate difficult emotions and relationships. Remember, healing is a process, and each step you take is significant in honoring your journey and finding peace amidst the turmoil.

NOTES

NOTES

NOTES

NOTES

NOTES

8

BETRAYAL AND REDEMPTION

This chapter centers on the profound and multifaceted experience of betrayal and the struggle for healing and justice in the wake of deep personal loss. This chapter delves into several interwoven themes:

1. **Betrayal and Deception**: The chapter vividly portrays the betrayal experienced by the protagonist, both from her late husband's actions and the deceitful behavior of those who should have offered support. The emotional weight of losing a loved one is compounded by the discovery of financial exploitation, infidelity, and a concerted effort by others to undermine her.

2. **Invasion of Privacy and Identity Theft:** The protagonist faces a severe invasion of her privacy, marked by the theft of personal documents and identity theft. This violation

exacerbates her grief and highlights the depth of betrayal she experiences from those who exploit her vulnerability for their gain.

3. **Spiritual and Emotional Conflict:** The protagonist's internal conflict between seeking justice and relying on her faith is a central theme. She is torn between the desire for retribution against those who have wronged her and a spiritual conviction that justice should be left to a higher power. This struggle reflects her broader journey of reconciling her faith with her personal suffering.

4. **Emotional and Financial Exploitation:** The chapter reveals how the protagonist's late husband's financial deceit and extramarital affairs contribute to her emotional and financial turmoil. The discovery of his secret financial dealings and the pawning of personal items underscores the depth of his betrayal.

5. **Spiritual Renewal and Healing:** Amidst the chaos and pain, the protagonist finds solace and strength through her faith. The support from her church and prophetic messages provide her with a sense of renewal and a path toward healing. This spiritual rejuvenation plays a crucial role in her journey toward reclaiming her self-worth and moving forward.

6. **Isolation and Self-Preservation:** The protagonist's decision to cut off contact with toxic influences and focus on protecting her family reflects a theme of self-preservation amidst betrayal. Her journey involves not only grappling with external conflicts but also finding ways to rebuild and protect her emotional and spiritual well-being.

In summary, Chapter 8 explores the deep impact of betrayal and deception on the protagonist's life, highlighting her struggle for justice, emotional healing, and spiritual renewal. It portrays a journey through grief and personal upheaval, ultimately focusing on reclaiming strength and faith amidst profound challenges.

DISCUSSION QUESTIONS

1. Personal Impact of Grief and Betrayal:

— How did the author's experiences with grief and betrayal shape her emotional state during and after the funeral? How did the external conflicts contribute to her internal struggles?

2. Family Dynamics:

— What do you think the author's experiences reveal about family dynamics in the wake of a loved one's death? How did her husband's family's actions affect the funeral proceedings and her personal grieving process?

3. Rumors and Miscommunication:

— How did rumors and false information impact the author's relationships with others and her ability to grieve? What strategies did she use to deal with the spread of misinformation?

4. The Role of Faith:

— How did the author's faith influence her decisions and responses to the betrayal and challenges she faced? How did Psalm 64 resonate with her situation, and how did it help her cope with the adversity?

5. Dealing with Identity Theft and Invasion of Privacy:

— How did the author handle the additional stress of identity theft and invasion of privacy? What might be some effective ways to cope with such situations while dealing with personal loss?

6. Navigating Relationships:

— How did the author's interactions with her husband's family and others reveal the complexities of maintaining relationships during times of crisis? What lessons can be learned about managing relationships when trust has been broken?

7. Feelings of Betrayal:

— How did the feelings of betrayal from her husband's family impact the author's view of her late husband and their relationship? How can such betrayals affect one's healing process?

8. Self-Care and Boundaries:

— What steps did the author take to protect her mental and emotional well-being amidst the chaos? How important is it to set boundaries and seek respite when dealing with multiple sources of stress?

9. Resilience and Redemption:

— In what ways did the author demonstrate resilience throughout her ordeal? How did she seek redemption and closure despite the numerous challenges she faced?

10. Reflecting on Personal Strength:

– How did the author's perception of her own strength change throughout the events described? How can one maintain a sense of self and strength when facing overwhelming situations?

These questions aim to facilitate a deeper exploration of the themes and personal experiences shared in Chapter 7, encouraging reflection and discussion on the various aspects of betrayal, grief, and redemption.

11. Understanding Betrayal and Trust

– How did the betrayal and deceit from those closest to the narrator impact their ability to trust others?

– In what ways can the betrayal described in this chapter affect someone's sense of security and well-being?

12. Handling Identity Theft and Financial Fraud

– How did the narrator's discovery of financial fraud and identity theft add to their emotional burden?

– What steps can someone take if they suspect their identity has been stolen, and how can they protect themselves from further damage?

13. Confronting the Past

– How did the narrator's realization about their late husband's behavior affect their perception of him and their relationship?

— How important is it to confront and process the painful aspects of a past relationship in order to heal?

14. Spiritual and Emotional Healing

— How did the pastor's words and the narrator's subsequent affirmations contribute to their emotional and spiritual healing?

— What is the significance of affirmations and positive declarations in overcoming trauma and moving forward?

15. Personal Growth and Resilience

— How did the narrator's experiences contribute to their personal growth and resilience?

— What can be learned from their journey about overcoming adversity and finding strength in the face of betrayal and loss?

16. Reflection on Forgiveness and Moving Forward

— How might the narrator approach forgiveness, both for themselves and for others who wronged them?

— What are some practical steps for moving forward after experiencing deep betrayal and emotional pain?

These questions can help facilitate a meaningful discussion about the various aspects of the narrator's experience and offer insights into dealing with similar situations in real life.

REFLECTIVE EXERCISE:
EXPLORING BETRAYAL, HEALING, AND REDEMPTION

PURPOSE:

This exercise invites readers to reflect on their own experiences of betrayal and the pathways to healing, helping them to process emotions and identify sources of strength.

INSTRUCTIONS:

1. Journaling Prompt:

— Reflect on a significant betrayal you've experienced. Write about:

— Your initial feelings and reactions when you discovered the betrayal.

— How this experience impacted your emotional state and sense of trust.

2. Recognizing Deception:

— Consider any instances where you felt deceived by someone you trusted. Write about:

— The signs you overlooked at the time and what you wish you had recognized.

— How this realization changed your perspective on the relationship.

3. Invasion of Privacy:

— Reflect on any experiences where you felt your privacy was invaded or your identity compromised. Write about:

- How this violation affected your sense of safety and trust.

- What steps you took to regain control and protect your personal space.

4. Spiritual Conflict:

- Explore the tension between seeking justice and relying on your faith. Write about:

- A situation where you felt torn between retribution and forgiveness.

- How your beliefs guided your response to this conflict.

5. Emotional and Financial Turmoil:

- Consider any moments of financial or emotional exploitation in your life. Write about:

- How these experiences contributed to feelings of vulnerability and loss.

- The ways you worked to reclaim your financial or emotional stability.

6. Finding Renewal:

- Reflect on how you've found solace and strength during difficult times. Write about:

- The sources of support you leaned on (friends, family, faith communities).

- Any practices or activities that helped you find peace and renewal.

7. Self-Preservation:

- Think about times you had to distance yourself from toxic influences. Write about:

— The feelings associated with this decision and the challenges it presented.

— How prioritizing your well-being impacted your healing journey.

8. Reclaiming Strength:

— Identify moments when you felt empowered to reclaim your sense of self. Write about:

— Specific actions you took to rebuild your life after betrayal.

— The personal strengths you discovered through adversity.

9. Affirming Your Journey:

— Write a personal affirmation that acknowledges your journey through betrayal and healing. Consider:

— What do you want to honor about your experience?

— How can you empower yourself to move forward with faith and resilience?

10. Setting Intentions:

— Conclude by outlining actionable steps you can take to continue your healing process. Consider:

— How can you cultivate supportive relationships and environments?

— What practices can you implement to foster emotional and spiritual well-being?

CLOSING:

As you reflect on these themes, recognize the complexity of navigating betrayal and the journey toward healing. Embrace the insights gained from your experiences and honor your resilience. Healing is a process that requires patience and self-compassion; each step you take is significant in reclaiming your strength and finding peace amidst the challenges.

NOTES

NOTES

NOTES

NOTES

NOTES

REVELATIONS AND REALIZATIONS: UNCOVERING THE TRUTH

The central theme of this chapter is the journey of self-discovery and liberation that follows the revelation of deep and unsettling truths about the protagonist's late husband. This chapter intricately explores several themes:

1. **Self-Discovery and Empowerment:** The protagonist's emotional journey is marked by a significant shift from grief and betrayal towards a sense of personal freedom and self-empowerment. Writing letters to her late husband serves as a therapeutic act, allowing her to express her pain and eventually find peace. This act symbolizes her process of letting go and reclaiming her own sense of self-worth and agency.

2. Uncovering Hidden Truths: The protagonist discovers troubling truths about her late husband's life, including his use of illicit drugs and financial deceit. This revelation is a pivotal moment, highlighting the extent of his deception and the impact it has on her understanding of their relationship and his true character.

3. Dealing with Betrayal and Misunderstanding: The protagonist navigates the complexities of familial relationships and the betrayal from her late husband's relatives. The chapter reveals the difficulties of dealing with false accusations and misunderstandings from family members who either mistreat her or offer belated support. This adds to her emotional burden but also underscores her resilience and ability to maintain boundaries.

4. Spiritual Insight and Acceptance: Throughout her turmoil, the protagonist seeks solace in her faith and finds comfort in spiritual guidance. This aspect of the chapter highlights her journey towards acceptance and healing, as she learns to reconcile her spiritual beliefs with the painful realities she faces.

5. Moving Forward and Rebuilding: The chapter portrays the protagonist's gradual transition from a state of distress to one of rebuilding and renewal. With the completion of legal and financial matters, she begins to focus on her future, symbolizing a new beginning and a move away from the trauma associated with her late husband's death.

In summary, Chapter 9 emphasizes the protagonist's path from profound grief and betrayal to a place of self-discovery, empowerment, and eventual acceptance. It explores the themes of uncovering hidden truths, navigating complex familial relationships, and finding solace and direction through faith and personal growth.

DISCUSSION QUESTIONS

1. The Therapeutic Power of Writing

— How did writing a letter to the narrator's late husband help in processing grief and unresolved issues?

— What other therapeutic practices might help individuals cope with unresolved emotions and find closure?

2. Understanding and Overcoming Self-Blame

— How does the narrator's shift from blaming themselves to finding freedom and self-empowerment reflect a journey towards healing?

— In what ways can individuals recognize and challenge self-blame in their own healing processes?

3. Dealing with Family Dynamics

— How did the interactions between the narrator's son and the late husband's relatives illustrate the complexities of family dynamics during times of trauma?

— What are some strategies for maintaining healthy boundaries with family members who may not support or understand your situation?

4. Navigating Grief and Family Relationships

— How did the narrator's experiences with her late husband's family affect her sense of closure and moving forward?

– What role can family members play in supporting someone who is grieving, and how can one address and manage family conflicts during this time?

5. The Impact of Dreams and Intuition

– How did the narrator's dreams and intuitive feelings contribute to uncovering truths about her late husband's life and death?

– How can dreams and intuition be used as tools for personal insight and understanding in difficult situations?

6. Understanding Substance Abuse and Its Effects

– How did the revelation of the substance abuse in the autopsy report impact the narrator and her sons' understanding of their late husband's life?

– What are some ways to address and cope with the impact of discovering a loved one's substance abuse after their death?

7. Legal and Financial Challenges

– What challenges did the narrator face in dealing with legal and financial matters following her husband's death?

– How can individuals effectively manage legal and financial responsibilities during times of personal crisis?

8. Finding Closure and Moving Forward

– How did the narrator's experiences with the autopsy report and the probate process contribute to her journey towards closure?

– What are some steps that can help someone move forward after dealing with complex and painful revelations about a deceased loved one?

9. The Role of Faith and Spiritual Guidance

– How did the narrator's faith and spiritual experiences help her navigate the difficult revelations and emotional turmoil?

– In what ways can faith and spiritual practices provide comfort and guidance during challenging times?

10. Self-Discovery and Empowerment

– How did the narrator's journey through grief, discovery, and legal battles lead to personal empowerment and self-discovery?

– What are some ways individuals can find empowerment and strength in their own journeys through grief and personal challenges?

These questions are designed to encourage reflection and discussion about the various themes and experiences presented in Chapter 9.

REFLECTIVE EXERCISES FOR CHAPTER 9:
"REVELATIONS AND REALIZATIONS: UNCOVERING THE TRUTH"

PURPOSE:

These exercises are designed to help readers process their experiences of self-discovery and empowerment, particularly in the context of uncovering difficult truths and moving towards healing.

INSTRUCTIONS:

1. Letter Writing:

– Write a letter to someone (alive or deceased) who has impacted your life in a significant way. In your letter, express your feelings about the truths you've uncovered regarding that relationship. Reflect on how those revelations have shaped your sense of self and your journey toward empowerment.

2. Self-Discovery Reflection:

– Create a list of personal qualities and strengths you've discovered about yourself through your struggles. For each quality, write a brief explanation of a specific situation where it was highlighted or tested.

3. Navigating Betrayal:

– Reflect on a time when you felt betrayed or misunderstood by someone close to you. Write about:

- The emotions you experienced during that time.

- How you navigated the complexities of that relationship and what boundaries you established.

4. Truths and Deceptions:

- Consider a truth you've uncovered about yourself or someone in your life that was difficult to accept. Write about:

- How this truth affected your understanding of your relationship with that person.

- Steps you took (or plan to take) to reconcile this truth with your reality.

5. Spiritual Insight:

- Reflect on how your spiritual beliefs have been tested during times of turmoil. Write about:

- A specific moment when your faith provided comfort or guidance.

- How this moment influenced your journey toward acceptance and healing.

6. Rebuilding Your Future:

- Imagine your ideal future three years from now. Write a detailed vision of what that looks like, including personal, emotional, and spiritual aspects. Consider:

- What steps you need to take to move toward this vision.

- How you can prioritize your well-being as you rebuild.

7. Empowerment Affirmations:

– Create a list of affirmations that resonate with your journey of empowerment. Write statements that affirm your strength, resilience, and ability to overcome challenges. Consider repeating these affirmations daily.

8. Boundary Setting:

– Reflect on a relationship where you need to establish or reinforce boundaries. Write about:

– The reasons for these boundaries.

– The steps you will take to communicate and maintain them.

9. Gratitude and Growth:

– Identify three things you are grateful for in your life right now, despite the challenges you've faced. Write about how these aspects have contributed to your personal growth and healing.

10. Vision Board:

– Create a vision board (either physically or digitally) that represents your goals and aspirations for the future. Include images, words, and symbols that inspire you and reflect your journey of self-discovery and empowerment.

CLOSING:

As you engage with these exercises, recognize the transformative power of uncovering truths and embracing self-discovery. Allow yourself the space to grieve, heal, and ultimately move forward with intention and hope. Your journey is unique, and each step you take toward understanding and empowerment is a vital part of reclaiming your life.

NOTES

NOTES

NOTES

NOTES

NOTES

NOTES

EMBRACING CHANGE: FINDING HOME IN UNEXPECTED PLACES

The central theme of this chapter is the transformative journey of healing and renewal through embracing change and finding new beginnings in the aftermath of loss. The chapter explores several interconnected themes:

1. **Emotional Healing and Closure**: The protagonist grapples with the lingering presence of her late husband and the emotional weight of his absence. The chapter portrays her efforts to find closure and peace, symbolized through her experiences with sensing her husband's presence and reflecting on their shared memories, including the poignant song lyrics that resonate with her sense of loss and the end of their relationship.

2. Spiritual Guidance and Transformation: The protagonist's decision to move is deeply influenced by her spiritual journey. Through prayer and fasting, she seeks divine guidance to find a new path for herself and her children. This quest for spiritual clarity reflects her desire to make decisions that align with her faith and to embrace a new chapter in her life with a sense of purpose.

3. Rediscovering Home and New Beginnings: The chapter highlights the protagonist's search for a new place to call home. Her journey to Atlanta and the sense of belonging she feels upon visiting different neighborhoods symbolize her quest for a fresh start. Finding a house that feels like home represents not just a physical relocation but an emotional and spiritual renewal.

4. Practical and Emotional Rebuilding: The practical steps of selling her old home, donating her late husband's belongings, and preparing for the move are interwoven with the protagonist's emotional process of letting go and moving forward. These actions reflect her commitment to starting anew and creating a positive future for herself and her children.

5. Faith and Providence: The successful outcome of her home search and the smooth transition process are viewed as manifestations of divine intervention. The protagonist's belief that these events are guided by God underscores the theme of faith and the idea that embracing change can lead to unexpected blessings and opportunities.

In summary, Chapter 10 emphasizes the protagonist's journey of healing and renewal through embracing change. It explores the themes of emotional closure, spiritual guidance, finding a new sense of home, and the practical aspects of rebuilding life after loss. The chapter conveys a message of hope and the potential for positive transformation even in the wake of profound grief.

DISCUSSION QUESTIONS

1. Experiencing the Presence of a Loved One

— How did the narrator's experiences of sensing her late husband's presence influence her feelings and decisions?

— Have you or someone you know experienced similar feelings of a loved one's presence after their passing? How did it affect you?

2. Symbolism in Music and Emotion

— What role did the song "Goodbye Love" play in the narrator's emotional journey and understanding of her relationship with her late husband?

— How can music or other forms of art help individuals process complex emotions related to loss and change?

3. Decision-Making After Loss

— How did the narrator's decision to move away and seek a new beginning reflect her process of healing and moving forward?

— What are some strategies for making major life decisions after experiencing a significant loss?

4. Spiritual Guidance and Decision-Making

— How did the narrator's spiritual fast and prayer influence her decision to relocate and find a new home?

– In what ways can spiritual practices or beliefs help guide individuals through difficult life transitions?

5. Finding a New Place to Call Home

– How did the narrator's experience of finding a new place to live contribute to her sense of starting fresh and finding a new home?

– What factors are important to consider when choosing a new place to live after a major life change?

6. Managing Practical Matters During Transitions

– What practical steps did the narrator take to manage the sale of her old home and the purchase of a new one?

– How can individuals effectively handle the logistical and emotional challenges involved in moving to a new home?

7. Emotional Impact of Relocation

– How did relocating to a new city impact the narrator's emotional well-being and her family's adjustment to the change?

– What are some ways to ease the emotional strain of moving and help family members adjust to a new environment?

8. Letting Go of the Past

— How did the narrator's decision to give away her late husband's tools and other belongings reflect her process of letting go and moving forward?

— What are some strategies for managing and letting go of possessions with emotional significance during a transition?

9. Support Systems During Major Changes

— How did the narrator's support network, including her church friend and real estate agent, contribute to her successful transition?

— What role do support systems play in managing major life changes, and how can individuals build and utilize these networks effectively?

10. Personal Growth and New Beginnings

— How did the narrator's journey through grief, decision-making, and relocation reflect her personal growth and readiness for new beginnings?

— What are some ways individuals can embrace personal growth and new opportunities after experiencing significant life changes?

These questions are designed to facilitate discussion and reflection on the themes of change, emotional processing, and personal growth explored in Chapter 10.

REFLECTIVE EXERCISE FOR CHAPTER 10: "EMBRACING CHANGE: FINDING HOME IN UNEXPECTED PLACES"

PURPOSE:

This exercise aims to help you reflect on your own experiences with change, healing, and the journey toward finding a new sense of home after loss or transition.

INSTRUCTIONS:

1. Guided Journaling:

– Reflect on a significant change you've experienced in your life. Write about:

– The emotions you felt during this transition.

– How you navigated the uncertainty and what coping mechanisms helped you.

2. Closure Letter:

– Write a letter to someone or something you need closure with (this could be a past relationship, a job, or a way of life). In the letter, express your feelings about the situation, what you learned, and how you plan to move forward. You don't have to send it; the act of writing can be healing.

3. Spiritual Reflection:

– Consider how your faith or spiritual beliefs have guided you through times of change. Write about:

— A specific moment when you felt spiritually supported during a difficult transition.

— How this guidance shaped your decisions and feelings about the future.

4. Vision for New Beginnings:

— Create a vision board that represents your hopes and aspirations for new beginnings. Include images, quotes, and symbols that resonate with your desire for transformation and renewal. Reflect on what each element represents for you.

5. Finding Home:

— Reflect on what "home" means to you. Write about:

— The qualities or feelings that make a place feel like home.

— Any physical spaces that have provided comfort during difficult times and how you can recreate that feeling in your current situation.

6. Letting Go Ritual:

— Design a personal ritual for letting go of the past. This could include:

— Writing down things you want to release on paper and safely burning it.

— Creating a physical representation of what you're letting go of and discarding it in a meaningful way.

— Reflect on how this act makes you feel and what you hope to invite into your life moving forward.

7. Gratitude List:

— Make a list of things you are grateful for in your life right now. Focus on aspects that have emerged from change or challenges. Reflect on how gratitude can shape your outlook as you embrace new beginnings.

8. Affirmations for Change:

— Write a list of affirmations that support your journey of embracing change. For example:

— "I am open to new beginnings."

— "I trust that I am being guided toward my best life."

— Read these affirmations daily to reinforce your commitment to transformation and healing.

9. Mapping Your Journey:

— Create a timeline of significant changes in your life. Mark key events, the emotions you felt, and how each change contributed to your growth. Reflect on patterns or lessons that emerge from this mapping.

10. Future Self Visualization:

— Take a moment to visualize your life a year from now. Picture yourself having embraced change and finding peace. Write about:

— What your life looks like.

— How you feel in this future self.

— Steps you can take today to move closer to this vision.

CLOSING:

As you engage with these exercises, remember that embracing change is a journey filled with opportunities for growth, healing, and rediscovery. Allow yourself the grace to process your feelings and to recognize that new beginnings can lead to unexpected joy and fulfillment. Your path is uniquely yours, and each step you take brings you closer to your true home.

NOTES

NOTES

NOTES

NOTES

NOTES

NOTES

FIVE YEARS LATER

The central theme of Chapter 11 is the transformative journey of healing from narcissistic abuse. The chapter reflects on the profound impact of betrayal and the complexities of recovering from emotional and psychological trauma. It emphasizes resilience, self-discovery, and the importance of seeking professional help.

KEY ELEMENTS INCLUDE

1. **Understanding Narcissism**: The author highlights the necessity of comprehending the traits and mechanisms of narcissistic personality disorder, which can help victims recognize their experiences and feel less isolated.

2. Emotional Recovery: The chapter explores the challenges of processing the emotional aftermath of abuse, revealing how the fog of the experience often obscures clarity until one is free from the toxic environment.

3. Forgiveness and Closure: A pivotal moment occurs when the author receives an apology from a family member, which validates their pain and aids in the healing process. Forgiveness emerges as a crucial element in releasing bitterness and fostering personal growth.

4. Empowerment and Growth: The author shares their journey of self-discovery, pursuing new interests, and building healthy relationships, illustrating how one can reclaim their identity after trauma.

5. Future Endeavors: The chapter concludes with the author's plans to write two new books aimed at supporting others who have faced similar challenges, emphasizing the importance of community and shared experiences in healing.

Overall, the chapter encapsulates the themes of resilience, the importance of understanding one's experiences, and the power of forgiveness as a pathway to healing and empowerment.

REFLECTIVE EXERCISE:
THE HEALING JOURNEY

1. Journaling Prompt:

— Take a moment to reflect on your own experiences with betrayal or emotional pain. Write about a specific incident that impacted you deeply. Consider the following questions:

— What emotions did this experience evoke?

— How did it affect your sense of self and your relationships with others?

2. Understanding Narcissism:

— Research and list some common traits of narcissistic behavior. Reflect on whether you've encountered these traits in your past relationships. Write down:

— How did these behaviors manifest?

— How did they make you feel at the time?

3. Recognizing Your Resilience:

— Think about the ways you have coped with your experiences. List the strategies you used to navigate your healing journey. Consider:

— What strengths did you discover within yourself?

— How did you find support (friends, therapy, community)?

4. Forgiveness and Closure:

— Reflect on the concept of forgiveness. Write about someone you need to forgive (this could be yourself or another person). Explore:

— What feelings are holding you back from forgiving?

— What would it mean for you to let go of this burden?

5. Setting Intentions for Growth:

— Think about your future and the person you want to become. Write down three intentions or goals that resonate with you as you continue your healing journey. These might include:

— Pursuing new interests

— Establishing healthy boundaries

— Engaging in community service or support groups

6. Visualizing Your Path Forward:

— Create a vision board or draw a mind map that represents your healing journey. Include images, words, and symbols that inspire you and reflect your aspirations for the future.

7. Sharing Your Story:

— If you feel comfortable, consider sharing a part of your story with someone you trust or within a support group. Reflect on how expressing your experiences can foster connection and healing.

REFLECTION:

After completing this exercise, take some time to review your responses. What insights did you gain about yourself? How do you feel about your journey moving forward?

This exercise can help you process your experiences, recognize your resilience, and set a clear path for healing and growth.

NOTES

NOTES

NOTES

NOTES

NOTES

NOTES

CONCLUSION

This final chapter reflects on the journey from loss to renewal, highlighting several key aspects:

1. **Transformation Through Grief**: The conclusion emphasizes how grief, while profoundly challenging, can lead to significant personal transformation. It portrays grief not as an end but as a transformative process that can shift despair into hope and darkness into light.

2. **Resilience and Strength**: The narrative celebrates the strength of the human spirit. It acknowledges the ability to endure hardship, find solace in small joys, and rebuild life even after experiencing profound loss. The protagonist's journey illustrates the resilience required to navigate through grief and emerge stronger.

3. **Renewed Hope and Faith**: The chapter underscores the role of time, faith, and perseverance in the healing process. It conveys how these elements contribute to finding renewed hope and strength, even as the pain of loss continues to resonate.

4. **Legacy and Cherished Memories**: The conclusion reflects on the lasting impact of the protagonist's late husband. It conveys that his memory and the lessons learned from his life

continue to guide and influence the protagonist, emphasizing the importance of cherishing and honoring the past.

5. **Support and Empathy:** The protagonist extends sympathy and support to others who have experienced grief, hoping that her story offers hope and reassurance. The conclusion acknowledges the shared human experience of loss and the comfort found in mutual support and understanding.

6. **Embracing Life's Paradoxes:** Finally, the conclusion highlights the paradox of life's dualities—joy and sorrow, love and loss. It suggests that within this paradox lies the profound beauty of existence and the continuous evolution of the human spirit.

In essence, the conclusion reinforces the idea that even in the face of profound loss, there is potential for renewal and growth. It celebrates the resilience of the human spirit and the power of faith and hope in navigating life's unpredictable journey.

FINDING CLOSURE AND EMPOWERMENT
THE JOURNEY BEYOND TILL BETRAYAL DO US PART

As we conclude our exploration of *Till Betrayal Do Us Part: A Memoir of Surviving Narcissistic Abuse*, we arrive at a moment of reflection and potential transformation. This study guide has been our companion in dissecting the raw and intimate experiences shared within the memoir, offering a space for dialogue, understanding, and healing. As we close this chapter, let us take a moment to reflect on the journey we have undertaken together and look ahead to the path of empowerment and renewal that lies before us.

EMBRACING THE LESSONS LEARNED

Through our discussions and reflections, we have delved into the intricate dynamics of narcissistic abuse, the profound impact it has on individuals and relationships, and the journey toward reclaiming one's sense of self. We have examined the memoir's powerful narrative, uncovering the strength and resilience that emerges from the darkest of experiences. The questions and exercises within this study guide have been crafted to help us process these lessons, and now it is time to integrate them into our lives.

1. **Acknowledging Growth**: Take a moment to recognize the personal growth you have achieved throughout this study. Reflect on the insights gained from the memoir and discussions, and acknowledge how they have shaped your understanding of yourself and your experiences. Growth often comes in subtle forms, and it is important to celebrate the progress made, no matter how small.

2. **Applying Insights**: The knowledge and wisdom acquired through this study are valuable tools for moving forward. Consider how you can apply the lessons learned to your daily life, relationships, and self-care practices. Whether it's setting healthy boundaries, practicing self-compassion, or seeking support, use these insights to foster a more empowered and resilient self.

3. **Continuing the Journey**: Healing and personal growth are ongoing processes. This study guide has provided a foundation, but the journey doesn't end here. Continue to explore, reflect, and seek support as needed. Engage in practices that nurture your well-being, and stay connected with communities or resources that offer guidance and understanding.

THE POWER OF SHARED EXPERIENCE

Throughout this study, the value of shared experience has been evident. Connecting with others who have navigated similar struggles provides comfort, validation, and strength. As you move forward, remember the importance of community and support. Whether through support groups, friendships, or professional counseling, maintaining connections with others who understand your journey can be a powerful source of encouragement and growth.

CARRYING FORWARD THE LEGACY

The memoir of *Till Betrayal Do Us Part* is not just a story of survival but a testament to the enduring spirit of those who face and overcome the challenges of narcissistic abuse.

As you close this study guide, carry forward the legacy of strength, resilience, and hope embodied in the memoir. Let it inspire you to embrace your own journey with courage and determination, knowing that you are not alone.

A FINAL NOTE OF ENCOURAGEMENT

As we part ways from this study, remember that the process of healing and transformation is unique to each individual. Embrace your journey with patience and self-compassion and honor the progress you have made. The memoir's message is one of hope and renewal, and it is a reminder that even in the face of betrayal and adversity, there is a path to reclaiming joy, love, and fulfillment.

Thank you for being part of this exploration and for contributing your insights and experiences. May you find peace in the knowledge that your journey, though challenging, has paved the way for a brighter and more empowered future.

MOVING FORWARD WITH HOPE

The end of this study guide marks not a conclusion, but the beginning of a new chapter in your life. As you step into this new phase, carry with you the lessons, strength, and hope cultivated through this journey. May your path be illuminated with resilience, and may you continue to embrace life with the wisdom and courage you have gained.

With heartfelt wishes for your continued growth and empowerment,

Author Cheryl Dyson-Bennett

RESOURCE PAGE FOR INDIVIDUALS EXPERIENCING NARCISSISTIC ABUSE

Navigating the complexities of narcissistic abuse can be challenging and isolating. However, support is available, and connecting with the right resources can provide crucial assistance and guidance. The following resource page is designed to offer a range of tools, support networks, and professional help to those who may be experiencing or recovering from narcissistic abuse.

1. Crisis Support

— National Domestic Violence Hotline

— Website: [TheHotline.org] (https://www.thehotline.org)

— Phone: 1-800-799-7233

— Text: Text "START" to 88788

— Description: Provides confidential support and resources for individuals experiencing domestic violence, including those who may be facing emotional abuse.

– National Suicide Prevention Lifeline

– Website: [988lifeline.org] (https://988lifeline.org)

– Phone: 988

– Description: Offers free and confidential support 24/7 for individuals in emotional distress or crisis.

2. Therapy and Counseling

– American Psychological Association (APA)

– Website: [APA.org](https://www.apa.org/helpcenter)

– Description: Provides a directory to find licensed psychologists and therapists in your area.

– Psychology Today Therapist Directory

– Website: [PsychologyToday.com] (https://www.psychologytoday.com/us/therapists)

– Description: A comprehensive directory to find therapists and counselors, including those specializing in trauma and narcissistic abuse.

– TherapyRoute.com

– Website: [TherapyRoute.com] (https://www.therapyroute.com)

– Description: An online directory of therapists, psychologists, and counselors, searchable by location and specialty.

3. Support Groups and Communities

— Narcissistic Abuse Recovery (Facebook Group)

— Website: [Facebook.com/groups/narcissisticabuse] (https://www.facebook.com/groups/narcissisticabuse)

— Description: An online support group where individuals can share experiences and support each other through the recovery process.

— Narcissistic Abuse Support Forum

— Website: [NarcissisticAbuse.com] (https://www.narcissisticabuse.com)

— Description: Offers a forum for discussions, support, and information about recovering from narcissistic abuse.

— Reddit: r/raisedbynarcissists

— Website: [Reddit.com/r/raisedbynarcissists](https://www.reddit.com/r/raisedbynarcissists/)

— Description: A subreddit for individuals who grew up with narcissistic parents, providing a space for discussion and support.

4. Educational Resources

— Books:

— "The Drama of the Gifted Child by Alice Miller

- "Narcissistic Abuse: Recovery from Narcissistic Abuse and Healing" by Jennifer Kromberg

- "Will I Ever Be Free of You?" by Karyl McBride

- Websites:

- Psych Central: Narcissistic Abuse [PsychCentral.com](https://psychcentral.com/lib/narcissistic-abuse)

- Mental Health America [MentalHealthAmerica.net](https://www.mentalhealthamerica.net)

- Narcissistic Abuse Recovery Program [NarcissisticAbuseRecoveryProgram.com](https://www.narcissisticabuserecoveryprogram.com)

5. Hotlines and Helplines

- SAMHSA's National Helpline

- Phone: 1-800-662-HELP (4357)

- Description: Provides confidential information and referrals for mental health and substance abuse services.

- RAINN (Rape, Abuse & Incest National Network)

- Website: [RAINN.org](https://www.rainn.org)

- Phone: 1-800-656-4673

— Description: Offers support for survivors of sexual violence, including emotional and psychological abuse.

6. Legal Resources

— Legal Aid Society

— Website: [LegalAid.org] (https://www.legalaid.org)

— Description: Provides free legal assistance and advocacy for individuals facing abuse and other legal issues.

— National Coalition Against Domestic Violence (NCADV)

— Website: [NCADV.org](https://www.ncadv.org)

— Description: Offers resources and support for individuals experiencing domestic violence, including legal resources and advocacy.

Remember: You Are Not Alone

Experiencing narcissistic abuse can be incredibly isolating, but support is available. These resources are here to offer you guidance, support, and a path to healing. Whether you are seeking immediate help, ongoing support, or educational materials, know that reaching out for help is a powerful step toward reclaiming your life and finding a place of peace and strength.

ABOUT THE AUTHOR

Dr. Cheryl Dyson-Bennett is a highly esteemed life coach, acclaimed author, and sought-after motivational speaker, dedicated to guiding individuals toward realizing their highest potential. As the visionary Chief Executive Officer of Designed for Greatness, LLC, and Women of Destiny Empowerment Enterprises, Cheryl leverages her extensive experience and passion for personal development to inspire transformative growth in others.

Cheryl's literary journey began with the release of her first book, In the Arms of Jesus: Favor, Increase and Promotion, in 2019, followed by the impactful Divine Keys to Unlocking Your Destiny. Since then, she has authored five additional books, each contributing to her mission of empowering and inspiring others. In addition to her books, Cheryl has created a plethora of journals designed to guide readers in their personal and spiritual growth, offering practical tools for reflection and self-discovery.

Her love for writing dates back to her childhood, when she would spend countless hours crafting stories and poems. Recognizing the profound power of her words to effect positive change, Cheryl pursued writing with a fervent dedication that has only deepened over time. Her works are infused with themes of hope, resilience, and divine guidance, drawing from her personal experiences and her unwavering belief in the power of faith and divine timing.

Cheryl's life mission is to empower women to navigate life's trials with grace and purpose, ultimately leading them to a fulfilling and purposeful existence. Her personal experiences with adversity have fortified her belief in the power of divine intervention and the importance of trusting in God's perfect timing. These challenges have not only strengthened her resolve but have also enriched her writing, making her messages of hope and transformation deeply impactful.

In addition to her roles as a life coach and author, Cheryl is a dynamic speaker who engages audiences with her heartfelt messages and practical wisdom. Her seminars and workshops have transformed the lives of many, equipping them with the tools and insights needed to overcome obstacles and seize opportunities.

Cheryl is also actively involved in various philanthropic initiatives, supporting causes related to women's empowerment and community development. Her commitment to giving back reflects her belief in the collective power of individuals to create positive change.

With an unwavering dedication to unlocking human potential, Dr. Cheryl Dyson-Bennett continues to inspire and uplift individuals, helping them navigate their journeys with confidence and purpose. Her work stands as a testament to the transformative power of faith, resilience, and the pursuit of greatness.

CHERYL DYSON-BENNETT'S PUBLICATIONS

In the Arms of Jesus: Favor, Increase, and Promotion

Divine Keys to Unlocking Your Destiny: A 30-Day Journey to Unlocking Your Destiny

Divine Keys to Letting Go: A Guide to Mastering and Unleashing
the Greatness in You, Let Go, and Take Charge of Your Life

Jesus Loves Me

Illuminating Your Path with God's Word: A 52-Guided Devotional to
Enlighten Your Journey through Daily Prayers and Confessions

Till Betrayal Do Us Part: A Memoir of Surviving Narcissistic Abuse

Journals

Pray, Trust, Wait, and Repeat

Divine Keys to Letting Go Prayer Journal

Anointed and Appointed Prayer Journal

I Am Blessed and Highly Favored Journal

Phenomenal Woman Prayer Journal

Stay tuned for Cheryl's upcoming book, *Moving Past the Hurt: Reclaiming Your Identity in Christ.*